The Soul Warrior

Four Powers to Unleash Your Entrepreneurial Drive

ABBOOD TAMIMI

PASSIONPRENEUR®
PUBLISHING

Publishing information
Publishing, design, and production facilitated by Passionpreneur Publishing,
A division of Passionpreneur Organization Pty Ltd, ABN: 48640637529

www.PassionpreneurPublishing.com
Melbourne, VIC | Australia

Dedication

To Mom and Dad
Thank you for your unconditional love and support.

Thank you for putting up with my crap. Thank you for your faith in me, even during those moments you knew I was going to fail; you were there to hold me when it happened. Thank you for teaching me values and strength. I'm really sorry you won't get to read this book, but I will tell you all about it when I see you in Heaven, In Sha' Allah (God Willing).

Introduction

*Spiritual warriors are courageous enough
to taste suffering and relate to their fear ...
suffering is not seen as a failure or
a punishment. It's purification.*

— *Sogyal Rinpoche*

ATTAINING FINANCIAL FREEDOM, being your own boss, and impacting people's lives — these are the outcomes that drive many aspiring entrepreneurs towards fulfilling their visions. Living a meaningful life by creating a legacy should always be the ultimate goal. While all entrepreneurs must strive to achieve their desires, not everyone starts out from the same place. As with any other group of people, many budding entrepreneurs go through this life suffering from the consequences of abuse. That was my story.

All people are created equal and free. It was meant to be this way since day one. Everyone is entitled to freedom, along with a set of supportive human rights that ensure equality and fair treatment. Unfortunately, there are many who have to fight to gain their stolen freedom back. They endure all sorts of abuse just to be recognized as human beings. They live in fear because they have lost the thing that matters to them the most — LIFE.

Abuse comes in many forms, and it doesn't discriminate — bullying, rape, abusive relationships, oppression, occupation, modern slavery, terrorism, racial profiling, or any atrocity that you can give a name to. Abuse divides people into two types — the oppressor and the victim. The more the victim surrenders to the oppressor's abusive "system," the more the victim's mind becomes "conditioned" to operate within it. Sadly, that's where many victims get stuck and surrender. The oppressor's "operating system" doesn't allow for self-liberation. That's when victims believe it's GAME OVER. Sometimes they refer to it as "destiny."

Does that sound familiar to you? If so, you will need to change that operating system altogether and adopt one that fosters freedom.

The truth is, sometimes oppression is external (i.e., done by other people) and sometimes it is internal (i.e., done by your own brain). The brain has its ways to create self-limiting beliefs; it articulates those beliefs and conditions, compelling our minds to accept them as true.

That was my mindset for over two decades. And in my years of struggle to get past it, I understood one thing — no one should endure abuse. It makes people's lives lose meaning. Nothing is worse than wondering why you were born and feeling you have to endure life.

Overcoming my limiting beliefs has given me clarity about my purpose. I connected with my soul and honored my inner call by creating a balance between four principal domains in my life — the spiritual, the emotional, the physical and the intellectual. This balance has allowed me to become the Co-Founder and CEO of 3mushrooms Telecom and the certified Executive Leadership Coach that I am today.

My experience with abuse has shown me that I contributed to enslaving myself by surrendering to my negatively charged mind. I always had the choice to challenge my thoughts, but I never did. Sometimes it was easier just to surrender and take on the victim role. It felt like "home." I came to realize that it was I who chose to live this way all these years, and that's when I started to do something about it.

The Soul Warrior talks about the four powers — faith, heart, health, and mind — that can help you become the entrepreneur you want to be. I will show you how to look at yourself through these four lenses to gain more clarity and create actions to start living an exciting life. You will use the power of faith to explore your spiritual domain to become familiar with your values and meet your inner leader. You will work on finding your life's purpose by learning how to answer your inner call and find your passion. You will also learn how to allow your soul to lead your life.

This book will also teach you to use the lens of compassion to explore the power of your heart. Examine your relationships. Evoke your empathy and extend yourself to be of service to those who need your help. This power shows you how to be a true human being by empowering your emotional domain.

And let's not forget the body. It is the physical machine that will allow you to carry your message and deliver it to the world. This book will also put that body on the treadmill and run some tune-ups so that you are physically ready for your journey. It's not only your mind that we are changing, but your appearance as well. The power of health is important to a more positive physical domain.

The intellectual lens, on the other hand, will help you find the learning opportunities that will help you attain your dreams. There is a lot of learning to do. Remember, it is a new operating system that you will be "installing." So, sharpen your MATRIX skills, because you will need all the knowledge you can get your hands on to further develop yourself. The power of mind is going to develop the intellectual domain.

The Soul Warrior is my mission to help as many people as I can and to liberate as many abused souls as I can. I want to help create a generation of free souls who have the vision and the will to become who they choose to be and live a purposeful and fulfilling life. I have managed to turn my suffering from abuse into a gift that I would like to present to you so that you can liberate your own soul.

With the help of this book, I want you to meet the future you, your inner leader, and evoke your sage powers. Do you know that you have those already? I also want you to experience life to its fullest and explore all the possibilities awaiting you. I want you to realize that you too are capable of living a life of choices. You are the only master of your destiny. Join me on this journey and let's explore the new you together.

You are a free human being. You are courageous to have endured life thus far with all its pains and with the weight you have been carrying on your shoulders. And you are still here — undefeated. There are no words to acknowledge how strong you have been able to survive this harsh life while still holding your head up. You are, indeed, a special soul. And for that, I commend you!

1
What does life mean to you?

*Challenging the meaning of life is the truest
expression of the state of being human.*

— Viktor Frankl

THE SHORTEST QUESTIONS can be the most difficult
to answer. Those about your existence are some of them.

I know what you might be thinking: this book is about
entrepreneurship, so why am I starting with questions
about life and existence? Well, before embarking on the
journey of entrepreneurship, it is necessary to understand
your life. This will give you clarity and insight into how you
should be contributing to the world.

While it is hard for people to agree on one single definition
of life, it is very important that you determine what life

means to *you*. Once you develop your own understanding of how life works, you will start to realize how you can be an effective part of it.

In his book *Man's Search for Meaning*, Viktor Frankl wrote about how he survived the German concentration camps. His story is far from happy — yet it is full of powerful ideas that challenge common conceptions about the meaning of life. Through his writing, Frankl reveals the power of having purpose — and that you *can* survive anything once you understand what your purpose is.

The truth is that everything is created for a purpose. If you reflect on the world around you, you will find that all elements were created for a reason. For instance, a tree has a purpose — it takes in carbon dioxide from the air and releases oxygen back into the atmosphere through the process of photosynthesis. It also provides shade, blocks the wind, provides shelter for birds and bears fruit to feed people — just to name a few of its purposes. Mountains play a role in shaping the weather, and they provide minerals for us to mine. The moon was created for a reason, as were the planets. Every single organ in our bodies was created to do a specific task. In other words, there is no random creation.

Consequently, your existence has a wisdom behind it. Your being on this Earth is not a coincidence. And when you are embarking on the journey of entrepreneurship, under-standing this wisdom will be the source of the clarity needed to create your future actions.

Finding one's purpose is a product of understanding how life works. It will also provide guidance as to where you should be heading.

Purpose and passion

In the process of discovering the meaning of life and finding your purpose, a new sense of desire will be born. Passion is the most critical element for your success. It is the guiding light that will illuminate your path in the darkest of nights. It is the source of strength that will give you the stamina to climb mountains.

Passion makes life rich. It keeps pushing you to learn more and more until you master your craft. It is a very powerful tool that can set you free to live a life that is worth living. In addition, doing what your heart desires is also linked to happiness. This is because happiness is based on a meaningful and purposeful life.

Jennifer Aaker and her colleagues at the Stanford Graduate School of Business published a study in the *Journal of Positive Psychology* focusing on how people spend their lives and what experiences they gain. They concluded that

"Happiness was linked to being a taker rather than a giver, whereas meaningfulness went with being a giver rather than a taker."[1]

Understanding what life means to you will give you a sense of purpose and direction, which in turn will reveal the "flame" necessary to live a life worth living to the fullest. While it is very important to understand life, find purpose, and discover what makes your heart beat faster, it is worth mentioning that not going through this journey has its drawbacks.

Can you imagine going through this life without having an objective or desire? What kind of future would this hold for you? One without direction, for sure. Living day after day without any sense of purpose will lead to a meaningless life — no legacy created, no memories, and no answers. Not having a purpose and passion means having no clarity and no direction in life.

My journey and meaning of life
Let me tell you my own story. The journey I have been on will help explain what life means to me, my purpose, and

---

1   Baumeister, Roy F., Kathleen D. Vohs, Jennifer L. Aaker, and Emily N. Garbinsky. "Some Key Differences between a Happy Life and a Meaningful Life." Taylor & Francis, August 20, 2013. https://www.tandfonline.com/doi/full/10.1080/17439760.2013.830764#preview.

how I found my passion. By doing this, I hope I will be able to inspire you to find your own ways, dictate your own destiny, and set yourself free.

Back in the 1980s in Doha, Qatar, between the ages of eleven and thirteen, I was gang-raped a few times — sometimes by two men and sometimes three. Those were the scariest three years of my life, EVER. Needless to say, those incidents put a dent in my childhood.

Seventeen minutes!!! It took just seventeen minutes to stop being a kid at eleven. And from that point forward, there was no going back. It was very painful — physically and psychologically. It was difficult for an eleven-year-old kid to handle. I was confused and lost; I was trapped in my own head. I could not understand what had happened, why it happened, why it kept on happening, or why it had to be me. I was very scared, in pain, and helpless. For three years, I was hostage to fear and a mere "boy toy" for the rapists.

After initially feeling confused about the whole ordeal, I started to feel fear creeping up on me. I felt like a kid who has lost his parents in a big marketplace, only it wasn't my parents I lost. It was something else. I couldn't get a grip on what exactly it was back then. All I knew was that it was a very scary thing to lose and even if I had my parents near and holding me, I was still scared to death — because

I didn't know what I had lost. Whatever it was, it took my life away from me. And I wanted it back!! At that point, nothing made me feel secure and I couldn't be alone for even a fraction of a second.

The whole thing escalated to another level: all those negative thoughts haunted my perception about myself. I felt I was not a man anymore. My manhood had been stolen from me. It didn't matter at this point whether or not I was a victim, because I had lost my "manhood" already. As the fear grew, it started to attack my spiritual beliefs about my creator, Allah (God). I remember the heated "dialogue" that I had with Allah, yelling and screaming at Him. I had a problem believing in Allah's mercy. How could He be merciful when He allowed those savages to attack an eleven-year-old kid? Where was the mercy in this? Where were you, Mr. Allah, when a child was molested in broad daylight!!? And you want me to pray to you? For what? For neglecting me? Not just once, not twice, not three times, and not four times. Five times!! And you call yourself "the Merciful"? Where is the wisdom in this?

It didn't stop at that. People needed to get a dose of my negativity, too. Why should they be off the hook when I was put through all that pain? People are not nice. I could not trust them. They only see what's good for themselves. They really don't care about how others feel, or what their actions lead to. *So why should I be a nice person?*

This is a little insight into the mindset of a rape victim. It starts with confusion, then fear takes over your body and brain; fear incubates anger — a lot of anger — and it turns you into a completely negative person.

It took me so many years to turn all that into a gift. Being raped can cause severe damage. There is nothing scarier than being lost in your own mind and losing faith and hope in people and in life. Rape has a special way of doing this to people. When I look back at my life and how I survived my trauma, I realize that the gift came from the way I handled my situation, often unintentionally.

For example, I buried myself at Dad's workplace when I was twelve. Why work? Because at work, Dad would be busy and would be very happy about my being there. He would spend time teaching me instead of asking me how I was doing. At work, I could avoid personal conversations and keep it "strictly business." The time I spent at Dad's business to escape my thoughts helped me develop my understanding of the business world at an early age.

So, when I was twelve years old, I knew how to operate the telex machine and how to use the typewriter in Dad's office. By thirteen, I knew how to write an invoice and write a receipt. I learned how to handle the cash register when I was fourteen. Every day I learned something that kept my thoughts away from what had happened to me.

Moreover, by reflecting on my past and looking at my trauma through an educational lens, I realize that I have learned many lessons because of my experience. The first lesson was how wrong it is to assume what people think. I learned this from my dad. He assumed I was okay when I was eleven. Never underestimate the brain of an eleven-year-old kid. Never underestimate the brain of any human being. Do not assume that you know, because we seldom do know what is going on inside someone else.

Another thing that made an impact on me as I was growing up was the British Council. If I wasn't in school or at Dad's work, I was at the British Council learning English. I saw it more as an escape from my suffering than an opportunity to learn another language. You see, it is easier to be alone among people you don't understand and who don't understand you. Learning English was a bonus. It was the only language spoken in the building where I sought refuge from my mind. Today, I'm writing a book in that language.

Escaping my reality and keeping myself busy, I was also able to develop this "fake character" to mask the person I felt I was, a social reject. Embracing this character for some years, I was able to cope with my life — not that this was necessarily the right way to do it. Reflecting on my life now, I realize that I've always had an ability to cope and adapt. I may have gotten some things wrong when I was a kid and didn't know any better, but at least

I have always been able to cope. It was just a matter of refining it.

I also understand now that if it weren't for my rape, I wouldn't be who I am today and I wouldn't know what I know today. That's how I was able to turn my trauma into a gift that has helped me to be of service to other people.

The breaking point

It was not until I was in my mid-thirties that I started to transform myself and think about the concept of *the meaning of life*. One day — and I remember that morning vividly — I woke up only to realize that I was hitting a wall. It was a horrible feeling, an unwelcome reality check! The clock was ticking, and I still hadn't done anything with my life. I felt like I was in this meaningless race with no destination, and I was running out of time. Then insecurity kicked in — the deadly combination of a sense of urgency and a lack of financial resources made my fear palpable.

Let me explain how I ended up in this state of mind. In 2007, I had to leave my banking career in Rhode Island, USA to move to Qatar to take over the family furniture business — Ghadeer Furniture — due to my father's deteriorating health. Being the oldest son in the family, this responsibility fell to me. The rest of my family members were residing in London, Ontario in Canada. My parents had travelled back and forth between Qatar and Canada.

When my father's health started going downhill, he decided to move to Canada for his medical treatment, which left me alone in Qatar running the family business. Well, at the beginning this sounded like a great opportunity to prove how good an entrepreneur I was. I wanted to see if I could apply what I had learned over seven years in the banking industry to the furniture business. I also thought the new experience would provide amazing opportunities to grow and learn.

Until 2010, everything was going fantastically. I managed to upgrade the business by redecorating the showroom inside and out. I introduced new processes and new software that would allow online accessibility and integration between the showroom, the warehouse, and the workshop. I managed to increase sales so much that we needed to upgrade the workshop. Everything was going according to plan, and I was really proud of myself.

Since I was living by myself in Qatar, I had no distractions and spent most of my time in the business. I was heavily involved in all aspects, which was good both for me and Ghadeer Furniture. After spending a couple of years setting up the business to be semi-automated, I decided to delegate tasks to new recruits.

This was toward the beginning of the boom in Qatar. Rents were skyrocketing and there was no government intervention to put a cap on the increase. Many businesses in

Qatar sponsor their foreign employees and, naturally, they take the responsibility for their accommodations as well. It's common for any business to have the rental burden of regular offices, showrooms, and the accommodation of employees who come to the country for work.

With most of their profits going toward paying rent, many of the small- to medium-size enterprises (SMEs) closed down. There was also a ban on certain Arab nationalities either entering the country on a visa or getting new work visas. Many foreign Arab employees were unwilling to go through the process of changing sponsorship to another employer, as rejection could lead to immediate deportation. So everyone was staying put; the Arab labor market had stalled and I was not able to hire anyone to handle sales and operation.

To make matters worse, the market situation for SMEs was very poor. There was little cash around. Though many businesses were forced to shut down, it didn't really affect the financially solid Qatari economy, which is heavily backed up by oil and natural gas, rather than local trade volume. Many people started to leave the country because they couldn't afford to live there any longer. Consequently, the SME sector was left to self-recycle, which contributed to the cash flow crisis. I had to lay off a couple of employees and had to live on US$1,500 per month in order to pay the remaining salaries and remain afloat.

That year my now late mother's health started to deterio-
rate as well. She had some medical tests done to explore
the possibility of coronary bypass surgery. After a discussion with me about her health and the situation ahead,
my father asked me to sell or liquidate the business. He
wouldn't be able to return due to his own health and
my mother's circumstances. The morning that followed
this discussion was one of mental paralysis; it brought
me down to my knees in tears. I felt so vulnerable and
empty. It was as if my dream of being an entrepreneur
were being taken away from me by force. All of those
images, those dreams of being successful, were shat-
tered in front of my eyes.

"Now what?" I asked myself. "What am I going to do next?"

And that was when I started to question my own existence.
Why was I here? Who was I living for? What did I want
from life? Was I living for myself or living a life centered
on taking care of my parents and not myself? How could I
combine the two? What was I supposed to do?

The only things I had back then were my own beliefs
and my soul — no money, no assets, and no ambitions. I
needed a break to rethink my situation. So I locked myself
in isolation for days, trying to regroup my thoughts, and
that is when everything started to change.

Looking within

Since I'm a spiritual person by nature, I always find comfort in reading my holy book, the Qur'an. During my period of isolation, I decided to spend more time with the Qur'an and seek comfort by being close to Allah.

But this time was different. I felt broken and humiliated, like I was drowning and needed help. So I started with the first chapter, or *sura* in Arabic, Al-Fatiha, and I decided to dig deep into it and study it further. This chapter, as short as it is, is referred to as "the mother of the book," "the mother of the Qur'an," "The Seven Highly Praised Ones," or "The Seven Repeated Verses." Al-Fatiha captures the entire essence of the Qur'an.

It is also worth mentioning that this chapter is recited at each of the five daily prayers for Muslims. Yet not many Muslims really understand the meanings embedded in those seven verses. I used to recite them in every prayer on a daily basis for years; I performed the prayers but really never bothered to think about what I was reciting. I was praying because it was my obligation as a Muslim to pray five times a day, not to meditate or to actually enjoy the spiritual benefits of praying. But now that I had decided to invest in my soul, I took a proactive approach and let my eyes, ears, and brain do their proper research. That's when the learning started for me.

Even though there's a lot of mind-blowing information in Al-Fatiha, I will only go through the parts that helped me find the meaning of life.

Al-Fatiha is exactly seven sentences:

1. In the name of Allah, the Entirely Merciful, the Especially Merciful.
2. [All] praise is [due] to Allah, Lord of the worlds.
3. The Entirely Merciful, the Especially Merciful.
4. Sovereign of the Day of Recompense.
5. It is You we worship and You we ask for help.
6. Guide us to the straight path.
7. The path of those upon whom You have bestowed favor, not of those who have evoked [Your] anger or of those who are astray.

— Al-Fatiha, the Holy Qur'an

After reading those seven sentences, I took a step back to decipher what I was reading. I looked at these seven verses in two parts:

1. From verses 1 to 6, it seems to me that the obvious is being stated. It's basically a recognition of Allah and His glory and that we worship Him.

2. There are three kinds of people described in verse number 7:

a. Those upon whom He has bestowed favor — who are those people and why them?
b. Those who have provoked His anger — who are those people and how do they provoke His anger?
c. Those who have gone astray — who are they and how did they get lost?

As I read the verses again, I became more curious and decided that I would research further to have a better understanding. So many questions kept coming out of nowhere. What makes those particular seven verses so important that we have to recite them in every prayer? Who are the three different kinds of people who are mentioned in the last verse? And so on. I wanted to find answers, so I let my mind loose and the rest followed.

My research has led me to the conclusion that Al-Fatiha actually consists of three parts. The first part is about the knowledge and recognition of Allah and His glory. This knowledge leads to the second part, which is action, the act of worshipping, and seeking His guidance. The last part talks about the relationship between knowledge and action and the three different outcomes. I have also found that when I recite Al-Fatiha, I'm actually engaging in a conversation with Allah Himself. Accordingly, there are two types of pairing here in the context of Al-Fatiha. The first form is pairing us — humans — with Allah. And the second form of pairing is between knowledge and action.

The first pairing form (between humans and Allah) gets clearer when we consider the Hadith (what prophet Mohammed [Peace be upon Him — PBUH] said Himself) about this kind of pairing. A prominent Muslim scholar named Abu Huraira has narrated the Hadith and said: *I heard the Messenger of Allah — Mohammed — (ﷺ) say: Recite Al Fatiha, for when the servant says: All the praises and thanks be to Allah, the Lord of all that exists.*

Allah says: 'My servant has praised Me.'

And when he — the servant — says: 'The Entirely Merciful, the Especially Merciful,'

Allah says: 'My servant has extolled Me.'

And when he says: 'Sovereign of the Day of Recompense (i.e., the Day of Resurrection),

Allah says: 'My servant has glorified Me.'

And when he says: 'It is You we worship and You we ask for help (for each and everything),'

Allah says: 'This is between Me and My servant, and My servant shall have what he has asked for.'

And when he says: 'Guide us to the straight path. The path of those upon whom You have

bestowed favor, not of those who have evoked
[Your] anger or of those who are astray,'

Allah says: 'This is for My servant, and My servant
shall have what he asked for.'

Part of the etiquette of reciting these seven verses is to
pause after reciting each one, because Allah is responding
to us every single time we recite them.

What? We are actually having a conversation with Him
and He dedicates His time to respond to us? WOW!
That was mind-blowing for me. It gave me a great
sense of comfort, as if I were in His presence and had
His attention. And since we have the ability to have a
conversation with Allah, then there must be more than
seven sentences we can talk about. So, in a way, the
Fatiha sets the tone for the entire Qur'an. The pairing
model of humans and Allah is carried out throughout
the entire book.

On the other hand, when we look at the pairing of knowledge and action, the description of the three kinds of
people becomes clearer.

1. The first group has knowledge and takes actions to
    spread that knowledge. This group is the one that is
    praised because they aim to contribute to humanity
    and make it better.

2. The second group has knowledge but doesn't do any-
    thing with it. Neither do they help themselves nor oth-
    ers. Those are the ones that provoke Allah's anger.
3. The last group acts without knowledge. This group
    is described by the word "astray."

Now, let's pay close attention to the first group — the
winners. Here you will find another form of subliminal pairing
as well. When you share knowledge and give unconditionally,
you hope for a better collective outcome. What I mean by
collective here is that there are two possible good outcomes
from giving. The first is the hope that your contribution will
benefit humanity. The second is the hope that you will win
paradise after your mission is over in this life. So there is a
benefit for society and a personal benefit. Hence, the word
collective. Both benefits, however, are based on hope. So, it
is safe to conclude that the act of giving is paired with hope.
For example, doctors give their medical expertise in the hope
that they will cure people. People manifest their knowledge
into new products hoping that they will help enhance human
life. When you give money to the needy you hope that it will
help them in some way.

Accordingly, by giving, the hope for a better outcome is
created. That was the "Aha!" moment for me. *Life is about
giving and hope.*

Another reassuring spiritual idea is found in what Jesus
taught about giving. "Each one must give as he has decided

in his heart, not reluctantly or under compulsion, for God loves a cheerful giver" (2 Corinthians 9:7 | ESV). This is a confirmation about the kind of people that Allah praises. All Abrahamic religions will agree on this fact. All of them teach us compassion and giving. That, for me, is pretty much the summary of what life means.

2
Why were you born?

*There is no greater gift you can give or receive
than to honor your calling. It's why you were
born. And how you become most truly alive.*

— *Oprah Winfrey*

AFTER REACHING THE rejuvenating moment of discovering my definition of life, a sense of purpose started to develop in me. I felt that I was on to something and became very observant of my own interests, my likes and dislikes, the whys and the hows. I was looking for the new me. My mission was discovering the giving part. What is it that I have to give? What is it that I like to do so much that can help other people? I felt like I couldn't even help myself, let alone help others. But I had to think harder and not give up, so I called my brother one day and I asked him, "What am I good for?" He replied, "Look back at your achievements and they will tell you." I liked the idea and my mind started heading in that direction.

When I thought about the greatest moments in my life, my teaching experience at the San Miguel School in Providence, Rhode Island popped into my head — it has a special place in my heart. In 1997, I was a student at the American University in Cairo (AUC); later, I transferred to Johnson and Wales University (JWU) in Providence, Rhode Island. During my first semester at JWU, I had to do community service as part of the bachelor's degree program. One of the opportunities was a teaching position at the San Miguel School, helping non-English-speaking students from grades five to eight improve their English and math skills. These students came from different cultural backgrounds, but they all struggled with the curriculum taught in English.

At first, I was scared. Only three years earlier, I had enrolled at the English Language Institute (ELI) at AUC to refine my English before I started my freshman year there. Now picture this: an international transfer student, in his first semester in the USA, in a city that he has never been to before is teaching English! Really? I remember being very hesitant to sign up for it, but now I'm so grateful I did.

The first day of class, I walked in, put my backpack on the table, and looked at the students. *A deer in the head-lights! Stand and Deliver*, an American film from 1988, was being played in front of my eyes. I was frozen until a kid decided to ask me where I was from because I looked "different" and had an accent. That question snapped me out of movie mode and I engaged in a conversation with the kid. From there, things started to get better. I started to gain confidence by telling them my own story and the struggles I had faced learning English. To my surprise, that had a huge impact on them. They knew that I understood and felt their struggle. Sharing my journey with them helped to establish trust between us; it allowed empathy and compassion to dictate my actions. That's how we connected.

One day that week, my supervisor asked me to give the kids a break and let them play American football. The kids were psyched! I was supposed to be the referee, but I had no clue about the sport — none whatsoever. So, I subtly approached my supervisor and told him that I was totally oblivious about American football. He looked at me, put his hand on my shoulder, and tapped it thrice. We looked at each other, then we both burst out laughing, and he left it at that.

"So, what am I gonna do now?" I asked myself. Being honest and humble was my first instinct. I gathered the kids and told them that I don't know anything about football. For some reason, that was wonderful news to them! They were so excited to teach me football. Not only that, they were so pumped to talk about the Patriots, an American football team representing the New England region. It was an opportunity for them to take on the teacher role. They proposed a deal. They would teach me football and I would teach them English. They got to do what they liked and I got to do with what I liked, and we would all grow together. A win-win situation. *How could you say no to that?*

I would get to learn while I taught.

Stepping up

By reflecting on that particular memory, I started to see that I have applied those skills in my professional career ever since. Empathy and compassion have helped me establish trust in business once my clients know that I understand their situations thoroughly. Trying to create win-win situations works wonders. This skill helped me become one of the top bankers in the region where I worked before moving back to Qatar.

Similarly, at Ghadeer Furniture, I made more sales simply by engaging with the customers to understand their situation before suggesting solutions. Understanding their feelings was vital. Empathy and compassion can uncover the underlying emotions that dictate decision-making. Once you understand people's true feelings and needs, you can create that win-win scenario.

By considering all these previous arguments, I was able to connect the dots and conclude that teaching was something I was good at. I find happiness in teaching. It is a form of giving and sharing my knowledge. By teaching, I don't necessarily mean being a schoolteacher or a university professor. It is more about empowering people with knowledge to help them make better decisions. That's why I like to teach; that statement summarizes my purpose. Not only is it compatible with my beliefs and Allah's teaching, but Allah blesses such deeds.

Once I reached that state of mind, a sense of clarity started to settle in. Now I knew what life meant to me. I also had an idea of what my aim in life could be. I became very excited. Just thinking about becoming an educator gave me butterflies in my stomach; it made my heart start pumping as if to confirm that I was on the right track. The more I thought about teaching and coaching, the more I started to focus on my purpose.

Taking the passion further
Naturally, when you have an interest in a subject, Mr. Google is happy to help. Thanks to Google social media tools, a prominent name in the coaching industry popped up on my Facebook page: Moustafa Hamawi, the Passionpreneur. After taking his online class on www.udemy.com, I decided to get in touch with him personally and have him as my coach. Once I spoke to Moustafa, I started to gain more clarity and more assurance about my passion and purpose.

There is really something magical about exploring your mind and heart. From that moment on, you perceive life differently. Your motivations change, your thoughts expand, and you head off in new directions. It is a complete overhaul, a truly rejuvenating path that is worth walking.

I had reached my initial goal of understanding life; I had found the wisdom behind my creation and what my heart desires. But I had not yet reached my destination. Other areas of my life were ready for my attention. I had to start with myself before I could offer myself to the world. I had to build my skills in order to be able to give better. I knew that the change in myself had to be comprehensive, but I had a huge appetite for learning. And I was hoping to create a change in this world and help abused souls set themselves free and enjoy the gift of life.

The support of a mentor in times of uneasy change
Now that I have explained how I managed to get some clarity about my existence, let me tell you that change is not easy. There were moments when I just felt lost, as if I were going around in circles. There were times when I didn't know how to deal with some specific issue, or simply how to get started. That's when having a mentor helps. A coach or a mentor is a sounding board, there for you when you need them, someone to help bounce ideas back and forth. Mentors hold you accountable for your progress. Don't try to do everything on your own; look for those

who have the knowledge to help you and team up with them. And remember, *when you don't know, just ask!*

Something else held me back, a thought lurking in the background: what if I try and fail again? Remember that there is always something positive in failure. It is called learning. You will never learn until you try. *Don't you agree?*

Failing is part of success. True failure only happens when you quit completely on your mission. But as long as you are still trying, it is called *learning*, not failing.

Likes versus passion
Another confusing scenario for me was differentiating between what I liked and thought I was passionate about, and what I was passionate about but thought I only liked. It is very important to realize the difference between the two. For example, I love cooking. I enjoy it because it makes people happy. Who doesn't like to eat, right? I like the idea of having a restaurant, but I am not necessarily passionate about it. In other words, just because I love cooking, that doesn't mean that I should be a restaurant owner. This form of passion can be a great business for chefs, but not for me. That's not how I see myself contributing to the world.

When you make a business out of something you're passionate about, you will use this passion to face any obstacle and fuel your determination to succeed. On the other hand, if you make a business out of something you only like, you lack the passion that makes you wake up every day to cause a change in this world. Some people are very clear about their passion; some people need reassurance, as I did; and others need help to discover what their passion is.

How do you find purpose?

There are many ways to get help in finding your purpose. The least you can do is to educate yourself more about the subject and read as much as you can. The internet is full of resources that are available to you for free. There are many books too that thoroughly address subjects you might be interested in. Grab some and read.

You can also start by questioning your belief system. Challenge yourself. Seek out religious scholars, university professors, and professionals and listen to their perceptions about life. There are also many entrepreneurial stories online. From them you can learn how successful people found their purpose and discovered what their passion is.

Guidance and assistance are very important throughout the journey. Having coaches and mentors in the past few years has taught me how to use my resources. Having someone with experience to show you the way is important because it will give you more confidence and clarity about your path. Try to look for a coach or a mentor in your network. Or ask someone successful to mentor you if they have the time.

3
The Power of Faith

*There are two "faiths" which can uphold
humans: faith in God and faith in oneself.
And these two faiths should exist side by side:
the first belongs to one's inner life, the second
to one's life in society.*

— *Maria Montessori*

IT IS VERY important to work on yourself because you
are the center of your existence. Before you start lifting
weights to shape the stunning body you want to have, you
need to work on the core muscles first. Similarly, to start
shaping your life the way you want it to be, you first need
to work on your core self.

Now, the core self includes four major powers that directly
affect the body and soul. These powers are *faith*, *heart*,

mind, and *health*. You need to master them in order to live effectively and happily. In this chapter, we will focus on the power of faith, which is the most important of the four. And as we move along, you will learn more about the other core powers and about ways to achieve mastery in them.

The power of faith

Faith doesn't necessarily mean believing in Allah or God. What I mean by faith in this context is the spiritual system that you believe in. You derive your principles from your value system and your personal beliefs.

Faith is your comfort zone. It's a place that you go to when life shuts its doors in your face. It is also a place where you find your purpose and renew your commitments toward developing yourself. You have to empower this aspect and make it solid because you will need it when you reach a vulnerable state of mind, as inevitably happens on any journey. It is a soft cushion to land on when you fall.

Faith is the gym that you use to exercise your soul. Questioning faith is your workout program. The more you question your faith, the more you can start believing out of conviction, and the stronger your faith becomes. Moreover, when you read and educate yourself more about your beliefs, you will find stories that will give you valuable lessons about life, and examples of leaders who embodied certain characteristics and principles that had led them to their success. By doing this, you also enrich your spiritual domain, and that will lead you to explore even more. It is hard to stop an inquisitive mind once it is hooked. Questioning and reading about your faith is the exercise that will grow your spiritual muscles.

Values and principles

Educating yourself about your beliefs and extracting values and principles from them gives you a moral compass. It is important to understand the difference between values and principles. Values are the qualities that dictate your behavior. Principles, on the other hand, are what dictate your actions. Let's say that you believe in the value of peace. Accordingly, being peaceful and choosing not to get involved in fights becomes your principle. If you believe in the value of honesty, then not lying becomes your principle. If you believe in integrity, then treating people with integrity becomes a principle, and so forth. Principles are used to calibrate your character so that it is aligned with your values, your compass heading, or your "true north," as Stephen Covey called it in his book *The 7 Habits of Highly Effective People*. Covey talks about the importance of living life based on character ethics that are, in turn, based on principles. It is an excellent book about personal change, one I recommend.

Spirituality and health

There was an interesting study, headed by Dr. Harold G. Koenig MD from Duke University Medical Center, that compared "the impact of spirituality and religiosity with other health interventions on mortality."[2] It found that "people with higher spirituality and religiosity had an 18 percent lower rate of mortality." It makes sense if you think about it. There are health benefits that come with the power of belief. Prayers, meditation, yoga, tai chi, or even some personal time with nature can help rejuvenate your blood flow and boost your immune system.

And since your core belief system is the place where you seek comfort, hope, and purpose, it can push depression away. It will take you out of your room to be part of a social network of like-minded people who embrace similar beliefs — and such people can help you empower those beliefs. You can find a social network that serves your divine world by going to a mosque, a church, a synagogue, a yoga class, a meditation class … you name it. Such a community can become your support group and the center of your ceremonial activities. In that sense, it's refreshing and prolongs your life.

2   Giancarlo Lucchetti, Alessandra L.G. Lucchetti, Harold G. Koenig, "Impact of Spirituality/Religiosity on Mortality: Comparison With Other Health Interventions," *EXPLORE*, Vol. 7, Iss. 4, (2011), Pages 234–238, http://www.sciencedirect.com/science/article/pii/S1550830711001029.

A broken spiritual system

On the flip side, a broken spiritual backbone can make it really difficult to handle or cope with some scenarios in your life. If your belief system is weak and cannot provide a sense of purpose, then why would you want to visit that place to seek guidance and direction? You can't give what you don't have, correct? If your divine beliefs have not been made solid through the challenging of your convictions, you cannot turn to them when you feel lost. To do you so will make you even more lost. Your spiritual muscles were never trained by questions. How can you expect performance from weak muscles?

It is crucial to learn how to believe. Faith is believing in something that you cannot prove — something that you choose to believe when the world cannot guarantee it for you. Belief will take you far in life even when everyone is telling you that you are heading in the wrong direction. If you learn how to do that, then you will be able to believe in yourself. Taking that journey with faith will help you discover the true you. Your brain will expand. You will know your qualities and capabilities. And once you develop that deep sense of your own convictions, making decisions about your life becomes a lot easier. You already know who you are and what you are capable of. You are now confident and determined, with a strong belief that you can work out difficulties.

Principles of character building

Let me walk you through a couple of scenarios so we can understand the dangers of not having a meaningful spiritual domain. When you live your life based on materialistic goals rather than principles, the lack or abundance of those materialistic factors can directly affect your emotions. What do I mean by this? If all that matters to you in life is making money, then the lack of it will make you miserable. Lack of money will make you feel insecure, but lots of money will make you sleep well at night. If you live for work, then being recognized for your effort will make you happy, while a lack of recognition will make you unhappy and perhaps depressed down the line. If your life is based on the validation of your friends, then having them around and caring about you makes you happy; if not, disappointment kicks in.

But what happens when you live your life based on principles such as integrity, proactivity, compassion, and empathy? At what point will any of those principles make you feel negative? The answer is probably NEVER. Have you ever heard the saying "never make decisions when you are angry and never make promises when you are happy?" That's because those actions are based on emotions. So, if your reason for living makes a yo-yo of your emotions, then how are you going to make the right decisions? On the other hand, if you live your life based on principles, then you will be emotionally solid; you will be in control — not controlled.

If your faith is not strong enough for you to handle the stress of life and its injustices, it is easier to drift into depression. It can eat your body alive and make you lose interest in life. Not having a strong and supportive belief system will make it harder to fight back, and you will be stuck, struggling to navigate through the consequences of not having a strong faith.

My spiritual journey

My journey with faith is deeply rooted in the Islamic school of thought. You should make your personal spiritual territory work for you in the same way. Regardless of what you believe in, make sure it helps you, not works against you. Your faith should be harmonious with your life and shouldn't conflict with it.

Among all the varieties in the spiritual buffet, I decided to go with a belief system that recognizes the existence of a Supreme Creator, as opposed to "nature." I'm convinced that there is a Supreme Being and He didn't create us haphazardly and aimlessly. That statement is unshakable for me because it works for me. I have no reason to make it stronger; it is just embedded in my DNA. I wanted to search for the wisdom behind my creation. There must be a way for that Higher Authority to communicate with us, to tell us what to do, since nothing in this universe was created for no reason, including humans.

My beliefs supported all Abrahamic religions (Islam, Christianity, and Judaism) since they address the same entity — Allah/God — which fits my definition of the Supreme Being. Any other ideology would not suffice for me. Now I needed to challenge these three religions and see which one I should eventually embrace. It was important for me to start by finding Allah first, before following whichever path my heart dictated. Accordingly, I questioned and researched these religions and eventually ended up back with Islam.

By doing my research, I was able to gather more knowledge about Islam. I know my resources and know how to access them. I also know what Allah means to me and how He plays a role in my life. I have become a believer out of conviction, not out of social conditioning. The more I researched, the more I connected with Him. I worship Allah not because it is an obligation; I worship Him because he is worthy of worshipping. That was the biggest shift during my spiritual journey.

Now, some of you may choose to avoid the monotheistic religions and go with nature or with any other spiritual entity that appeals to you. That is fine. Whatever works for you. The point here is to establish faith, not to preach about a specific one.

During my isolation period in my house in Qatar, I had the chance to work on my faith and my core beliefs. When I approached the Qur'an with an open mind, I guess I was trying to find the answers to my situation. I was trying to understand how it could possibly be merciful. I was so angry that I had a confrontation with Allah and I let it all out. I was furious and I was yelling, asking Allah what else He wanted from me. "You want me to pray, I do, and I try my best to do them all every day. You want me to fast; I fast during Ramadan (the Holy month of fasting) and more. You asked me to give alms when I can, and I do when I can. I also read my Qur'an. I try to be a good person every day. Is this all not enough? And what do I get from You in return? A MISERABLE LIFE! And then You tell me that You love me?? Explain that!! Where is the wisdom in that?" Picture a madman, locked in a house by himself, yelling and screaming these things at the walls. That was me!

I was mentally drained, tired, and hopeless. But I felt that I could not just give up. I had already hit rock bottom. It really could not get any worse than this. So I chose to be strong-willed and change my situation. That's when the first word that was revealed in the Qur'an suddenly popped into my head, out of nowhere. The word is "READ." That inner voice is what made me read the first chapter of the Qur'an, the Al-Fatiha. Once I researched the three kinds of people (that I have mentioned in an earlier chapter) and the concept of pairing knowledge with action, I concentrated on the first kind — those who have the knowledge and act. "Who fits into this category that I can learn from?" I asked myself. The most obvious answer was all the prophets. There were two factors particularly relevant to my interest:

1. All Abrahamic religions come from the same source, Allah/God, whom we all pray to. Accordingly, Allah's message is consistent, and all prophets complement each other.
2. We have access to information about Mohammed (PBUH), Jesus (PBUH), and Moses (PBUH).

These two facts made it easier for me to read about these three leaders and extract some of the common qualities that had made them successful. Why these three individuals in particular and why not any other political figures or prominent businessmen? Because these three are the epitome of faith.

These three figures share many qualities. The most interesting is that they all went to the same school, the "International School of Shepherds." As a matter of fact, there is no prophet that Allah has sent to humanity who was not a shepherd.[3] Abu Huraira reported in a Hadith that "the Prophet, peace and blessings be upon him, said, 'Allah did not send any prophet but that he cared for sheep.' The companions asked, 'And you as well?' The Prophet said, 'Yes. I was a shepherd with a modest wage on behalf of the people of Mecca.'"

---

3   "Did All Prophets Work As Shepherds?" Questions On Islam, https://questionsonislam.com/question/did-all-prophets-work-shepherds.

I found this very interesting; it made me curious as to why herding sheep is a big deal. So what did I do? I read!

The wisdom behind herding sheep

The following is a quote from an article on www.question-sonislam.com:

Herding sheep is for practicing about running the business of ummah (people) and gaining experience, for dealing with sheep improves emotions like leniency and compassion. When the prophets show patience during herding sheep and picking them up after their scattering on grassland, transporting them from one grassland to another, protecting them from wild animals and thieves around, and when they see and experience the differences in the nature of animals, how they disagree with one another in spite of their weaknesses and being in need of getting on well, they become familiar with showing patience for their ummah (people) and understand the changes in their nature and differences in their minds. So, they show mercy to the weak ummah, wrap their wounds and treat them well. After all, those who herd sheep can tolerate the challenges of these kinds of attitude far more easily than sudden starters. However, this virtue is gradually gained by herding sheep.

Sheep are more vulnerable than other animals; and they scatter more easily than camels or cattle, which can be tied with ropes. Sheep obey orders more readily even though they scatter more easily.

The three prophets needed the qualities described to help them with their missions. They needed the patience to be resilient, the compassion to master leadership, and the empathy (towards the weak) to gain respect and trust.

From an entrepreneurial point of view, these three men had a certain belief — let's call it the "business idea"; they embraced certain common qualities, lived their lives based on universal values and principles such as love, trust, honesty, integrity, empathy, compassion, and much more, and they were not interested in materialistic gains whatsoever. They lived for their purpose, not for themselves. They wanted to change humanity and make it better. They wanted to provide guidance, the "service," that would show humankind how to lead a successful life by following their paths. Even today, thousands of years after they left us, people are still using their "service." That's the legacy that each one of them has created.

We all know that financial gain was not the aim for any of the three prophets. But there were entrepreneurial lessons that I wanted to extract from this spiritual domain. I knew that living life based on principles was very important, but how was that going to make people believe in me and my business? I reversed the question and asked myself: Why am I following Mohammed? Why do I believe in Jesus and Moses? Was it because of who they were, or was it the content of the message itself that provided me with the power of belief?

Thinking deeper about it, I reached the conclusion that it was the message that made me a believer, not the prophets. The reason I believe in the message is that it provides value to my life. It provides answers to life. It guides humans and acts as a frame of reference when one is in doubt. Based on this insight, I concluded that people believe when they see value. That's why they believed in the prophets. They provided value to humanity. That was an eye-opener for me.

Value and identity

To succeed, you need to offer value, not products or services. The product or service exists to deliver value. That's why people buy them or subscribe to them.

Moreover, delivering value is what helps identify the person who is delivering it. For example, do you know the difference between an apple tree and an orange tree when they are not bearing fruit? Possibly not. But would it be easier for you to identify the trees if they *were* bearing fruit? Absolutely. Why is that? Because the human brain is hardwired to spot values. Fruits provide value to people. An orange, for example, is a source of food. It is also a source of vitamin C. It makes for a great orange juice for your breakfast and it can be an amazing sorbet on a hot summer day. You can also use the fruit to make orange cakes for birthdays or make some Chinese orange chicken for dinner when friends come over. Do you see what happens? Have you realized how many possible outcomes are generated once you spot just one value?? An orange tree is identified by the oranges it bears. Similarly, you — as a person — will be identified based on the value you provide.

The picture was getting richer with the knowledge I had accumulated. So far, I had learned how to find meaning in life and to find my purpose; I had decided to live my life based on principles and had used those principles to deliver the values of my purpose. This is the general picture that I started to embrace to develop new skills and put them into a working business. I was preparing the proper ground to transform the old me into the new *super* me.

Entrepreneurship starts with one's self. That's why I decided to work on myself before becoming more effective in helping others. I needed to learn how to help myself first.

Cause and effect
Once I understood the pairing concept discussed in Chapter 1, life's dynamics became easier to grasp. Pairing is the essence of life. It explains life in the context of cause and effect. It empowers Newton's third law: *For every*

action, there is an equal and opposite reaction. If you put in the effort, you will reap the benefits. To create life, you need a pairing of knowledge and action. Consequently, an action is paired with a reaction.

That made me realize that the situation I was in was a reaction to an action in the past. So what was that action? Using the concept of pairing, I came to find out that it was the lack of a sense of purpose and consequently of direction. I didn't choose to be miserable, but if I had never worked on myself in a way to ensure success, why should I expect a different outcome? I also realized that my efforts in the past had had no direction. I had no idea who I wanted to be, so I could not align my thoughts and actions to be that character I longed for. I had the "generic dreams" that everyone has — being successful, living a happy life, or being rich. They were very broad. There was nothing unique about my dreams. It was not surprising that I ended up where I did. Simply put, without clarity I had no direction — another example of pairing.

My faith became stronger because I started to believe. I started to believe because I wrestled with my faith. I hammered my holy book, the Qur'an. I didn't surrender to the "this is how I was born" mentality. I didn't want to be Muslim because my parents were Muslim. So I kept on reading, questioning, doubting, and reflecting — and this holy book still stands correct to me. It has answers to my questions about life. It is in perfect harmony with science and it proves it too. It shows the secrets of how nature works and how we should comply with it. It shows how we are all spiritual beings in human forms. It elevates my thoughts, broadens my horizon, encourages me to question before I believe.

It challenges me, and the more I challenge it back, the more proofs I find. The knowledge I get from this book is what motivates me to learn. The more I learn, the more I'm able to do, and the closer I come to my objective. Like the domino effect, one brings the other. That's when I truly became a believer out of conviction.

I have a place to go to that will fuel me with all the knowledge and strength I need when life gets tough. It is a place that comforts me, a place where I can have my own conversation with my Creator. In this domain I get to vent, confess, cry, and seek help. This is a place where I know for a fact that He is listening and He will help, that He knows everything, and He accepts me for who I am. He loves me and wants the best for me. He guides me and He answers back in His own way. This feeling of being connected to a higher power gives me all the strength and confidence I need.

Communicating with the Supreme Power

You might be wondering how Allah responds when you converse with Him, right? Well, thanks to Facebook and Google AdWords, I can explain that feeling now. Have you ever had a conversation with a friend or typed something to find on Google and a Facebook-related advertisement pops up on your Facebook page? Freaky, isn't it? Well, Allah works in similar ways. He simply sends thoughts into my head that pop up out of nowhere. My gut feeling, which is my notification center, tells me that I have just received a message from Allah. Sometimes, gut feelings occur without messages. Sometimes, things don't go as expected, but later you find out that it was an act from Allah. This process is really hard to explain but the Google AdWords and Facebook mechanism is the closest analogy. If computers can do it, then rest assured that Allah can do more than that.

Everything I have learned has helped me develop self-confidence. I'm a firm believer in cause and effect, in the pairing concept, in the value of living life because you have a purpose and a mission to fulfill. It is a fact that if you put in the effort, you will reap the benefits. It is only a matter of time. Regardless of how much I fail, eventually it will pay off, as long as I keep on trying and perfecting my methods. There is nothing to lose. And fear only exists because I chose to allow it to exist. Fear is my worst enemy, the one that would hold me back. But I realized that it is my choice to cause the action and live the reaction. It is my choice to choose optimism and hang on to facts, not fictitious fear. Positivity and hopefulness became my tools, which helped in developing the second part of the faith cycle — faith in myself.

Faith, a choice

Now I understand that faith is a choice. And with that choice, I can build an impactful future, one that will hopefully provide value to serve all human beings.

I chose to happen to life instead of waiting for life to happen to me. By believing in my choice, I started to feel the newly born flame in my heart lighting up my brain. Mahatma Gandhi said, "A man is but the product of his own thoughts. What he thinks, he becomes." There are hundreds of motivational quotes from various leaders out there. They all agree on the same principle — that the power of faith can take you a long way.

The application of faith in life

Now let's talk about the application of my faith in my life and how it has changed my thoughts and behavior. I was able to find my purpose by reading more about my three leaders of choice. My purpose is to liberate people who are suffering from abuse of any sort and educate them so they can make better decisions about their lives or their business, so they can live the life they dream about. Some of the qualities that I have extracted from these leaders are honesty, proactivity, compassion, giving without expectation, integrity, synergy, responsibility, adaptability, being fair, and many more.

I examined each quality to see where I stood with them in all aspects of my life, the physical, social, spiritual, or intellectual. For example, let's consider honesty and my desire to be a man of integrity. Looking at honesty from a physical perspective, I would ask myself, am I honest with my health? Is being overweight healthy for me? Am I acting with integrity toward my own body? Am I taking care of it? Looking at it from the social aspect, I would wonder, am I honest with myself? With my family, friends, or coworkers? Do I come across as a man of integrity to them? From a spiritual aspect, I ask, am I honest with my beliefs? Am I honest with Allah? Am I honest in the way I live my life and interact with nature? Am I honoring my value system and living by it? And lastly, from the intellectual perspective: do I give my brain the chance to grow and allow it to expand? Have I acquired my knowledge the proper way — a way that is credible and trustworthy?

The need to evolve started to rise in me with these questions. I realized that there were many behaviors I needed to stop, or acquire, or change, or develop to align myself with my new values. Once I began working on myself, I knew the outcome would be great. I was excited to "build" my new character.

I am constantly developing, enhancing, and shaping that character — that person that I aim to be. I have faith that things will work out, but I can't succeed just by thinking about it. I have to do something about it. My daily plan has turned into an execution plan, because I now know what I need to do to fulfill my purpose.

I educate myself every day about my work, my industry, my niche, my competition and about business trends — because that's what is expected from me as an educator and consultant. My purpose, to educate, backed up with a strong "I can do it" conviction and an appetite to learn have been dictating my decisions on a daily basis. Will this move make me a better educator? Does it conflict with my principles? Is the outcome going to be something I strive for? These are the questions I ask myself, and everything has become clearer, and prioritization has become easier due to this clarity. That happens when you let faith take its natural course. Your behavior changes.

The significance of the spiritual domain

The spiritual realm is extremely important. It provides directions to your moral compass. Yes, it is not easy to knock on that divine door, as it requires a deep examination of your most profound beliefs and your perception about life. I understand that.

People can be hesitant about confronting their beliefs; they are afraid doing so will make them anxious. So they avoid it altogether. Lots of things make it difficult for people to explore this realm and enjoy its findings. For instance, some people always think about God when you say the word spirituality. That word gets mixed with religion, since religion is a form of spirituality, but there can be faith and spirituality without religion. There are other ways to achieve a strong belief system. Find something that is appealing to you.

On the other hand, there are people who believe that religion is evil and it causes people to kill each other. Well, let's think about this for a minute. People don't blame physics as a branch of science for the bombing of Hiroshima and Nagasaki; they blame those who hijacked the laws of physics to kill people. People don't blame chemistry when chemical weapons are being used; they blame the group who used the laws of chemistry to hurt people. People don't blame engineering for designing tanks, nuclear submarines, stealth fighters, or other war machines; they blame those who use those machines. Only religion gets blamed for disasters that were created by its hijackers. Why is that?

Let's suppose that you do believe religion is evil. Have you done due diligence to verify this piece of information from credible sources before accepting it as a proven fact, as opposed to mere opinion? We all have responsibilities toward our own beliefs. We have to be honest with ourselves to believe with conviction. That doesn't happen by listening and repeating what other people say. Conviction demands validation. If you are not convinced, you will not believe.

Some will point out that there are people who are successful but not necessarily spiritual. Let's examine this thought for a minute. First of all, you don't need spirituality to learn how to do business. The point here is to find a way to sharpen your ability to believe so you can believe in yourself. Successful people believe in themselves. Faith can help with this.

Moreover, "me time" can be a spiritual experience if one chooses it to be. Those successful people might be spiritual in ways that may not be categorized under spirituality according to your frame of reference. It can be a simple moment of reflection, a moment of counting blessings or a moment to connect with one's soul to seek clarity. All those are considered spiritual activities.

Now you have an idea about how faith works. You can see how important it is to empower your spiritual domain to find your purpose and to extract values and principles to live by. You can see the role faith plays in developing your principles further to create a character that will deliver the value of your purpose. It is your time now to start working on your own faith and to prepare it for the journey ahead of you.

Start by questioning. Go to your group leader, whether an imam, a priest, a rabbi or whoever is a good fit to represent your faith, and question them and educate yourself further about your beliefs. And once you start to form a divine system, make sure that you actually practice it. That's how you exercise your soul, by praying and meditating — or by walking in nature, if that's where you get your spiritual strength.

Try to discover yourself in this aspect of life, and the more you question, the more you will believe. Put it into practice, embrace it in your daily life, and block some time for it on your daily calendar.

4

The Power of the Heart

The believers, in their love, mercy and com-
passion for each other, are like a single body;
if one part of it feels pain, the whole body
responds to it with wakefulness and fever.

— Prophet Muhammad (PBUH)
Sahih al-Bukhari (6011) and Sahih Muslim (2586)

I HAD DEFINED the purpose of my soul; I was also able to define the principles by which my new character would live and the values that it would deliver. It was wonderful. But to regulate this character and align it with my moral compass, I needed to use my heart. The same applies to you.

The power of the heart will help regulate the way you love yourself, your family, your partner, your friends, your colleagues, your coworkers, your future clients, your neighbors, your society, and, eventually, the whole world. Your heart is the lens through which you will be able to see and understand people better. It is also the tool that can help filter your emotions to maintain your sanity.

I believe that with our hearts we can achieve miracles. Just like any other organ in our bodies, and just like everything that is created in this life, the heart has a purpose. It's the source of life and where the soul resides. The heart possesses so many different dimensions that are deeply rooted in all human interactions. There are so many benefits and values that we can acquire and develop simply by listening to our hearts.

The heart and compassion

For me, the heart is where we learn compassion. Compassion is a universal value shared by many belief systems. It is also an integral part of many traditions, ethical systems, and religions. For example, in the Bible, we can find many examples that promote love and compassion. "The Lord is gracious and compassionate, slow to anger and rich in love. The Lord is good to all; He has compassion on all He has made" (Psalm 145:8–9). The Jewish faith preaches this value. Rabbi Hillel once described the Jewish faith by saying, "That which is hateful to you, do not do to your neighbor. That is the Torah — and everything else is only commentary."

The Golden Rule: "Do unto others as you would have them do unto you," also promotes kindness. The Dalai Lama, one of the important monks from the Gelug School, the newest school of Tibetan Buddhism, puts it subtly by saying, "My religion is kindness." In Islam, the teaching of compassion is apparent in many verses in the Qur'an. "Those who believe and do good deeds — the Gracious God will create love in their hearts" (Qur'an 19:97). The reward for the good deed is to receive love. If Allah is giving us love as a reward, should we not pay attention to the power of this gift? It is clear that love is a divine quality that is essential to becoming an empathetic human being. Love also lives in your heart and it will only shine in as much space as you give it to shine. But once you embrace it and allow it to take over, the word 'shining' is inadequate to describe its power.

Moreover, the heart is a powerful tool that helps you step out of your comfort zone and your personal frame of reference — to extend yourself, listen with empathy, read between the lines, and profoundly understand and feel for other human beings without compromising what you stand for. By being compassionate, you develop a stronger sense of understanding and appreciation of people for who they are, what they do, what they go through, what they believe in, and what their needs are — without judgments and perceptions of your own. Once you do that, trust will instantly be established and communications will become more fluid. It will also enable you to be a key player in creating change in their lives.

The heart has its own way of enhancing social relationships. Powerful principles, such as acts of philanthropy,
volunteer work, or even embracing a loving and caring
personality can be achieved if we make compassion
a core value. Kindness and a tender heart can create
win-win scenarios in all your professional and social
arenas. That's the essence of success. It can also elevate
and enrich your social relationships and positively shape
your character.

The heart and fulfillment

The heart is also a place that gives you a sense of security
and a strong sense of fulfillment. Our social and emotional
intelligence is shaped by our social relationships and our
emotional life, among other factors.

By nature, we are social beings. We are part of a bigger
picture. We were not created to live in isolation, but to
form a society and work together for a better life. We
have to interact with each other to resolve problems,
discuss ideas, work on projects, and so many other things.
Remember, the heart is a tool to help you extend yourself to deeply understand others. A sense of security
will develop from knowing that your aim is to create a
beneficial scenario for those with whom you interact, one
where both individuals flourish. Once again, we call this a
win-win scenario.

A sense of security also stems from the confidence that you can serve others in creative and collaborative ways, knowing that your effort will result in a positive change in someone's life. Whether you serve through your work, through volunteering or through any other forms, the objective at this point is about blessing other people's lives as opposed to seeking recognition. N. Eldon Tanner once said, "Service is the rent we pay for the privilege of living on this Earth."

The heart and health

It should not be surprising to learn that the power of the heart has a positive and healing impact on one's health. One study conducted by researchers at the Stanford University School of Medicine found that a warm, fuzzy feeling creates the same response in the brain as painkillers, without the harmful side effects.[4] "When people are in this passionate, all-consuming phase of love, there are significant alterations in their mood that are impacting their experience of pain," writes Sean Mackey, MD, PhD, Chief of the Division of Pain Management, Associate Professor of Anesthesia and senior author of the study.

---

4   Sean Mackey, "Viewing Pictures of a Romantic Partner Reduces Experimental Pain: Involvement of Neural Reward Systems," *PLoS ONE,* Vol. 5 (October 10), https://www.researchgate.net/publication/47520879_Viewing_Pictures_of_a_Romantic_Partner_Reduces_Experimental_Pain_Involvement_of_Neural_Reward_Systems.

"We are beginning to tease apart some of these reward systems in the brain and how they influence pain. These are very deep, old systems in our brain that involve dopamine — a primary neurotransmitter that influences mood, reward and motivation." While doctors are not ready to tell their patients to ditch their pain medication and revert to love as the first line of defense, the study suggests that the area in the brain that handles and reduces pain is the same area that is activated when experiencing love.

Emotional stability

When your actions are based on love and compassion, they will automatically direct your intentions to the person you are serving. You focus on the other person's feelings and emotions instead of your own. As a consequence, your emotional state will be stable and solid, because it is the other who needs to be heard, not you. You will feel fulfillment because you are answering your inner call. Unconcerned about your own emotions, you can serve the other person better. That's where fulfillment comes from — by being on purpose.

So, open your heart and use it to serve people in creative, collaborative, and tender ways. Regulating your heart will give you control over your emotions and will help you make better decisions.

What happens when you don't have compassion?

If you take love out of your heart, the heart will only be concerned about its own well-being, not others'. This can only result in selfishness, which will negatively affect your character. Lack of kindness is not highly regarded in any society. And when the heart can only see itself, people around you will be able to see that as well. Actions will speak out louder. It is not hard to tell who is selfish and who is generous. So how do people in your culture perceive selfish individuals? I'm sure it is not going to be a positive image, to say the least.

Another disadvantage of not having compassion is losing opportunities to develop meaningful relationships. Whether on a personal level or a professional level, people connect a lot quicker with a compassionate heart. It allows for an open and a clear line of communication that will make relationships healthy. You will not be able to create those types of meaningful relationships with your clients/customers, suppliers/vendors, investors/stakeholders, or your team, if you don't extend your heart to them. Without compassion, developing mutually beneficial relationships can be challenging.

Living a life without compassion will lead to insensitivity because you cannot extend your heart to listen to another person's needs or problems. This will hinder your ability to help them. What I mean by "listening" in this context is the empathetic type of listening. Empathy is a consequence of compassion. When you don't listen with your heart, the other person will know it. It is very easy to perceive who is sensitive and who is not.

Everyone knows how it feels when you talk to a cold person as opposed to a warm person. It isn't rocket science. People use their own emotional intelligence to evaluate various relationships and situations. For example, have you ever been in a room full of strangers and suddenly felt that one of them just radiates positive energy and fills the space? This happens because your heart picked up some signals from that person that communicates care to others. They are very connected to people around them without even needing to say a word. This is compassion in action!

What people see and notice is the way you present yourself, your smile, your welcoming and loving attitude. All this is based on compassion. And if there is no place for kindness in your heart, then people will quickly start to see that. This will allow them to assume things about you, and, slowly, you will find them drifting away from you.

Compassion summons humanity

We all have obligations toward ourselves, the society we live in, and the environment that we live in. We use our value system to define the ways through which we can contribute and make an impact on the world. The Dalai

Lama expressed his thoughts about kindness being a basic human quality by saying, "At the level of our basic humanness there is no source of conflict. Basic human nature is compassion. This is logical because we were born from our mother and were nurtured by her affection and care." On the other hand, if you consider our political environment nowadays, you will find that many human beings have been displaced, refused asylum, banned as immigrants, killed by gun violence, murdered in schools and churches, and been exposed to so many other disturbing scenarios. The common characteristic that has allowed this to happen is a lack of sympathy. The lack of a tender heart strips the quality of being human away from anyone. So the question is, do you want to be human or part of the animal kingdom? Compassion is the differentiating factor here.

I came to learn the impact of kindness at a later stage in my life. Back in 2012, I met with Themis Violaris, who is my current business partner to discuss an opportunity in the telecommunication sector in the maritime industry in Bahrain. After working together to execute our plan — a headquarter in Cyprus with commercial entities in the Arabian Gulf region — we both decided to embrace compassion as one of the core values of 3mushrooms Telecom. We are constantly working on finding opportunities to enrich this value and make it better and more effective. It is an ongoing learning process that enriches our positive emotions. You will find a sense of fulfillment and purpose once you start seeing life through a soft lens.

Let me share some other experiences that helped me realize the importance of this value in my life. It is hard for me to write about my philanthropic acts because they are not meant to be known — let alone bragged about in a book. But I feel it is necessary to use one example from my personal life to help make my point. A few years ago, I decided to find opportunities to develop and empower my heart because that's where leadership comes from. By educating myself more about the topic, I was able to find many ways to develop my compassion. In 2015, during Eid Al Adha — a religious Muslim holiday and a Christmas-like holiday for the kids — my brother, my business partner, and I went to a toy shop in Limassol, Cyprus and bought hundreds of toys as holiday presents. We then went to the Red Cross to pass on the toys to kids who had fled the Syrian war and ended up in refugee camps in Cyprus. We didn't believe that any kid should go through Eid without a toy, so we presented them with some. We gave them hope. We gave them love and a sense of belonging.

A palpable gap gets filled and an immense sense of achievement descends the minute you know that you have caused happiness in someone else's life. Nothing beats that feeling, NOTHING! A small gesture like passing out toys made the kids happy. So, later that year, we collected clothes and returned to the Red Cross because winter was approaching and the refugees needed clothes. And there was that unbeatable feeling again!

Powerful positive emotions are born during the act of philanthropy. I became addicted to this feeling and started to do other things that provided this happiness; it made me evolve more and more. Through philanthropy, I started to believe in my purpose more strongly. That's how I ended up learning about coaching. It is just another way to help people with diverse needs, although it works in a completely different way. Instead of helping people with money and clothes, I can help them by sharing what I know. Hopefully, by educating them, I will have helped them to generate the money necessary to afford their dreams. It is as if one act leads to another.

Using brotherly love has also made an impact on my company's performance. At 3mushrooms, compassion is the core value on which we base our SELF-EVALUATION system. My teammates set their personal and financial growth plans and I help link their job's outcome to their plans and coach them along the way. Every quarter, we sit together and discuss how much closer each teammate is to his goals and how the company can help him move forward. It's all about them, their goals, their livelihood.

They get to evaluate themselves, but not based on the company's goals. The company's goals are communicated and achieved differently. This is very different from my previous experience in the banking industry, where all evaluations were geared toward increasing the bank's profitability. My performance was measured by how much money I brought to the bank. If I met my financial goals, then I had value and I got a "bonus." They didn't really care about my personal goals, which meant a lot more to me than the bank's goals. Had they paid attention to them, I probably would have worked a lot harder and been more loyal to the bank. But banks are too material-istic to be considerate.

I didn't want my new teammates to feel the way I felt in the bank, yet the company still needs to meet its goals. Introducing the self-evaluation system and showing team-mates how it helps them achieve their goals, we saw an increased input level at work. It was the natural result. Why? Simply because their job has become meaningful to them. It gets them closer to their dreams. Everyone who works at 3mushrooms has a personal plan to help them grow. No one should come to work not knowing why.

The self-evaluation system
It takes time to start a business, acquire people, and find a way to create an environment where people are working toward the same goal. A good evaluation system, one that makes sense, first has to offer value to the teammates so that it can create an impact on their performance. This thought is compatible with my personal belief that life is about giving and hope, and it is compatible with the name and the philosophy of 3mushrooms. Why mushrooms? Mushrooms usually grow in clusters and troops. Seldom

will you find a mushroom growing by itself. The co-growth concept of mushrooms is the base of my business philosophy. *You grow, I grow, and anyone who will be dealing with us ought to grow with us as a consequence.* Similarly, the self-evaluation system has to foster growth before it measures performance.

How did I establish that? By ridding myself of any personal or company interests and concentrating on the interests of my teammates and their lives in general. When you pay attention to your teammates and extend yourself to learn more about them as people, you can easily establish strong connections and establish trust, because the other person knows that you are doing this for him. It's just like conversations with your doctor regarding your medical issues. When you visit your physician, you naturally talk about your symptoms, your experience with illness, your limitations, your objectives and ways to go about reaching them; you create a plan to get healthier. This is because you trust that doctor to help you. You commit to the plan because of this trust. That level of trust and commitment was what I was after. So I started to get an idea about the evaluation system in my mind. I needed to empower my teammates' lives to gain commitment from them.

So what does the evaluation system at 3mushrooms look like? It starts with the teammate, their life, their family, their wants, their needs, their ambitions, and where and what they want to be in the future. All of this has nothing to do with the company. Once I get to know what their direction is, I take that to the next level. I ask them, "How are you going to achieve that?" And the more they talk about their thought process, the more I think about how 3mushrooms can help them achieve that and how they can capitalize on the opportunity presented and where it will take us both.

For example, during one evaluation, a teammate expressed his passion for technology. He said that he liked working at 3mushrooms because it offered him the opportunity to help people working with the sea. He also had an idea about an invention that he wanted to develop on his own. So I asked him questions about where he wanted to go with that and what it meant to him to do such a thing, and what values he'd get by offering his knowledge or inventing his own solution. He said that it would bring more revenue to the company and that would make him happy. I then asked him how it would help his wife and family and make them happy at home. He was surprised to hear that question because he couldn't connect the dots. When he asked me what I meant by that question, I told him that this evaluation was about him — his life — not mine, not the company's. I explained to him how he can also make his family happy by starting the new project and being a partner in the project with 3mushrooms. I told him it would be like starting a new small business within 3mushrooms itself and that the newly born company would be a partnership between him and 3mushrooms and he would get to share the revenue generated for the sales of his new invention. By showing him how he can grow and enjoy the benefits of being a business partner and how his family can enjoy more benefits from the extra revenue that will be generated, I helped the light bulb begin to shine in his mind.

Now, as you read this, we have three new inventions that have come from our teammates, and they have become partners in their own businesses. They win and, naturally, 3mushrooms wins too. I gained the commitments I needed and I achieved a win-win scenario — 3mushrooms started to achieve seven-digit numbers in sales every year. This was all a result of a considerate evaluation system that is designed to help teammates grow in their personal and professional life first, before they have an impact on the company's performance. Everyone gets a piece of the pie here; it's large enough for everyone to share. This kind of compassionate system will allow you to concentrate on the lives of your teammates; by understanding them better you can help in making them better. But if you keep telling your teammates how they should develop skills to benefit the company's performance, neglecting their own lives, you will not go anywhere.

Compassion is the key
Compassion is a necessity for success and a vital quality for any human being. There can never be any negative outcome when your actions are based on love. It is a

powerful tool that can elevate your life and add extra meaning to your purpose. What you should know is that this power of the heart can be developed more easily than any of the many other tasks you will go through when you embark on your entrepreneurial journey. I say it is easy because it requires you to connect with your basic humanity. So don't feel discouraged if you don't know where to start or how to find opportunities that will offer this training to you. Start by going to a mosque, a church, the Red Cross, the Red Crescent, an orphanage, a refugee camp, a shelter, or even look for homeless people in the street and offer something — clothes you don't use, an extra dollar, or even a cup of coffee. Whatever you have, begin with it. Small and consistent acts can have a great impact — more than you might ever think. Just start and the rest will follow.

Some might argue that there are many successful businesses out there that are not based on compassion. Well, what kind of success are we talking about here? Monetary success?

If the aim is to just make money then, yes, you can achieve that. But without considerate and compassionate leadership, I doubt that any business will continue succeeding for a long time. Employee retention is going to be difficult due to a lack of fellowship. Employees quit their jobs because of management, not because they are not qualified. They don't feel appreciated. A "successful" company with unhappy employees is not really what I call successful.

Sales figures are not a true measurement of success in my book. It's like gambling. Today you might be lucky and sell big. Tomorrow you may suffer because an employee left due to a lack of warm-hearted leadership. And that's not how success is defined.

Some people believe that the world has changed and it is hard to find good people. The golden rule of "doing unto others as you would have them do unto you" is hard to implement because so many people today are not worthy of it.

This is a dangerous assumption to make. It means that you are giving up hope on helping others who might need help the most. There is always a motive behind any behavior, good or bad. Assuming that some people are not worthy of compassion can — in some scenarios — lead to their death. To give you an example, let's talk about police brutality in the United States. How many cases have we seen of civilians being brutally shot dead by police officers without any justification? Why did that happen? Because the police officer didn't have a tender heart. There were no signs of consideration in the behavior of the cops who took the lives of innocent people just because they thought the victim was holding a gun. That's an act of someone who is trained to fear, suspect, and shoot. They concentrate more on their own safety than on the safety of the civilians they are supposed to serve and protect.

Just imagine, what would happen if these police officers were to extend their hearts and show some empathy to their victims? At the minimum, they would still be alive with us; they would have had a second chance in life. But that didn't happen. Now you can see how important it is to be kindhearted even when you think the person in front of you doesn't deserve it. You can't know what's happening in their minds or what makes them behave in a particular way unless you listen empathetically, with your heart. That's when you can correct, improve, and empower someone else's life. It can be a turning point for them.

Developing a sense of compassion

There is no doubt that practicing love can be very difficult. It is hard to be compassionate when our mental state does not want to allow us to do so. Sometimes we feel exhausted, a little low, sick, or we need some tender love and care ourselves. Even then, it is necessary to adhere to your values and principles — because they make you who you are and who you will be. You have to be consistent in your behavior, whether you are sick or tired or out of sorts. Here is what I want you to do to start developing your heart power.

The process

The first thing you can do is to start educating yourself about love. There are many resources out there to help you learn about the topic. You can find classes to attend — both online and offline. Find a role model who represents compassion for you and learn from him or her. Study their behavior in depth, discover the consequences of their kind behavior and learn from them. Your goal is to reaffirm the value of love in your entire belief system. Once you start to understand how compassion works, apply that to yourself and your social relationships.

Start with yourself. Think of a friend who came to you in a time of need, asking for help. Think about your reaction, your behavior; think about how you extended yourself to understand your friend better so you could help them. Now think about times where you were struggling yourself and how you reacted to yourself and how you treated yourself. You will probably find a difference between the two reactions. We usually look down on ourselves when we make mistakes; we believe that we got ourselves into this struggle, so it makes sense to be harsh on ourselves. Does that sound familiar to you? If so, well, you need to stop doing that. Learn how to love yourself, learn how to be kind to yourself. Don't judge yourself; be kind. Befriend yourself. Give yourself a break and switch to the mentality of "I will learn from this" to create positive thoughts. It is your choice.

The day has twenty-four hours, and they will pass whether we like it or not. Whatever we do within these twenty-four hours is entirely our choice. You can spend it crying over yourself or loving yourself and making it better. It's your choice!!

Find a picture of yourself when you were a kid, young enough to be innocent and worry-free. Look at the picture; you will see the true essence of yourself. Look at that kid — examine the innocence, the vulnerability, the need for help, the tenderness; think of all the love that child deserves and treat yourself the same way you would treat that child. Think of that kid making the same mistake you just made. What would you tell them? I doubt you'll hammer the kid for their mistake. No, you'd realize there was something that the child needed to learn and that's why they didn't succeed. That's how we treat kids. With love and compassion. Treat yourself the same way.

Once you start getting the hang of this soft quality and adopt it as a core value in your life, start practicing it on your old, broken relationships. Reach out to the people concerned and see if you can sit down and talk about it. This is when you let the other person do all the talking and you do all the listening, with your heart.

Always remember, it is not about you, so your opinions shouldn't surface before this stage. And once you know the other person's position, summarize your understanding back to them to reaffirm it. If you were spot on with your summary, then move toward creating a win-win situation with them. And when you establish that, you naturally become a leader, perhaps without even realizing it.

Just keep doing it, even when it gets hard. Your values and principles are the most important things you have. Whatever happens, never let them go!

5
The Power of Health

Exercise is the key not only to
physical health but to peace of mind.

— Nelson Mandela

WE HAVE A saying in the Middle East that goes like this: *The right mind is in the right body.* I'm sure this is a universal statement, and every culture has its own ways of expressing the same concept. It is hard to find anyone who doubts the benefits of a physical workout. Body fitness is vital to living longer so you can enjoy and maintain an awesome life. Exercising is not going to make you successful; it's the consequences of the exercise that will help you reach success. It is the habits that you will develop through exercising — such as commitment and organization — that will help you through the rocky road of entrepreneurship. Also consider the benefits you will reap when you make your heart and body stronger. It helps you endure difficulties in life and combats disease that might slow you down or — God forbid — take your life away.

On the other hand, let's consider Chris Farley, John Candy, Patrice O'Neil, Big Punisher, James Gandolfini, or Elvis Presley, to name a few. While all these celebrities were very successful, they all died young (less than forty-five years old) and they were all obese. The reason for their obesity? Lack of exercise. Their bodies couldn't overcome the conditions they were struggling with. If you are planning to be successful, you might as well plan to live long enough to enjoy it.

The positives of exercising

Let's discover some of the positive qualities of training and see how it can affect your life.

Endurance

Endurance — in simple terms — is the ability to withstand a challenge, whether it is physical or mental. Since we are talking about fitness, let's pretend you've signed up to run a marathon. Before the challenge, you will need to go through endurance training. This is achieved by doing cardiovascular exercises to make your heart stronger and able to pump more blood through your body. The heart is a muscle that cannot be directly trained at the gym, but you can train it by working on the larger muscles group, such as your legs. Running, walking, cycling, and jogging can increase your cardiovascular efficiency. Endurance will teach you how to go through hardship, knowing that with this pain you will grow, just like your muscles. You will learn to push harder rather than quit early. This is an important quality to have because life has many challenges. You will need endurance to be ready physically and mentally to face them.

Flexibility

Another quality that comes with endurance is flexibility. You can achieve this by stretching. It goes without saying that you need to warm up before a workout and cool down after you finish. You stretch your muscles to warm up, release tension, and stimulate blood circulation in preparation for a tougher exercise regime. After the workout, stretching is necessary because it brings more oxygen into your muscles and prevents lactic acid build-up. Lactic acid build-up is what causes the pain and stiffness that you feel after the workout program. Stretching helps relieve that.

Strength

Strength is another benefit of physical exercise. This happens when you do muscle resistance training like push-ups, pull-ups, sit-ups, and weightlifting. Whether you train to be a bodybuilder or to have lean muscles is entirely up to you. It makes sense that you should put more effort into strength training if you are doing labor-intensive work. But if you have an office job, then a toned body with lean muscles should be fine. The choice is yours, but they both have good outcomes.

So how do you build strength? It is common to see people in the gym lifting weights and pushing themselves until they look like they can't do it anymore. Yet they keep doing it until their muscles rupture. When muscle ruptures, the body registers pain, but when the muscle's fibers regrow in forty-eight hours, they grow stronger. This is the basic theory behind muscle strength. Building more strength requires great patience and endurance. As an entrepreneur, there will be times where you feel that your patience is running out. Muscle-strength training will teach you how to be more patient.

Boosting brainpower

From a broader perspective, body exercise can also boost your brainpower. John F. Kennedy once said, "Physical fitness is not only one of the most important keys to a healthy body, it is the basis of dynamic and creative intellectual activity."

In her article "5 Mental Benefits of Exercise," Dr. Shawna Charles, a psychologist, says that physical training can develop intelligence and strengthen memory. A study conducted on mice and humans also shows that a cardiovascular workout creates new brain cells through a process called neurogenesis, which improves brain efficiency. It also prevents memory loss by empowering the hippocampus, the part of the brain responsible for learning and memory. Other studies have shown that exercising has an impact on creativity and mental energy.

Quality sleep

Another benefit of a workout program is that it can help you relax and improve your quality of sleep. When we work out, our body temperature increases due to faster blood circulation. This can have a calming effect on the brain, which will lead to a much more comfortable sleep. Dr. Charles says, "Exercise also helps regulate your circadian rhythm, our bodies' built-in alarm clock that controls when we feel tired and when we feel alert." Even though exercising is great, it is recommended that you avoid doing it right before bedtime.

Now that we have looked at some of the many benefits of being active, it is logical to assume that there are disadvantages to being lazy.

Disadvantages of physical inactivity

Choosing not to train can have a damaging effect on both your body and mind. Obesity is just one of the possible results of a sedentary lifestyle.

Cardiovascular diseases

Lack of training can lead to cardiovascular diseases (CVD), which can lead to premature death. If we look at the independent factors for CVD — such as obesity and the development of diabetes and hypertension, for example — you will find that all of these can be eliminated with physical exercise.

Lack of activity can contribute to high blood pressure and elevated cholesterol levels as well, which are also considered major factors affecting mortality. It is scientifically proven that exercising is a way to prevent a first cardiac episode and is useful to help patients' recovery from coronary surgeries. Not exercising means you are exposing yourself to variables that can affect your health.

Cancer risks

Not only can physical inactivity promote cardiovascular diseases, but it also increases the exposure of the human body to various types of cancers. An interesting and thorough report published by the World Cancer Research Fund and the American Institute of Cancer Research (*Diet, Nutrition, Physical Activity and Cancer: A Global Perspective*), suggests that "physical activity has an effect on several bodily systems including endocrinologic, immunologic and metabolic processes which can, in turn, affect the risk of development of several cancers." Working out has effects, to varying degrees, on different types of cancer. You can find the report at www.wcrf.org/dietandcancer/.

From obesity to diabetes — the scary condition

If obesity increases the risk of diabetes, then think about the lifestyle that comes with such a condition. It is hard to stick to a diabetic-friendly diet for the rest of your life, and it will also make life less enjoyable. Going out to eat with your friends can be quite a challenge. And just imagine the number of shelves in the supermarkets filled with products made with processed food and sugar! The diabetic patient might spend their life popping pills simply to overcome the symptoms these products cause, rather than treating the core problem.

Until you change the way you look at your food intake and exercise, you will feel constraints in your life. Even if you are obese and not diabetic, you will always face a challenge shopping for clothes. Your shopping will be based on what's available in 2XL, 3XL, 4XL, etc., rather than having the option to choose what you actually like. Obesity and diabetes can seriously restrict what life has to offer. I don't believe this can be classified as a "happy life."

Effects on mental health

In addition to all these physical issues, a sedentary life-style can take a toll on mental health as well. We feel fatigued when we get sick. Our mood changes when we get a cold or flu simply because we feel "out of it." I'm sure you have heard the expression "I'm not a good patient." Can you imagine what would happen if you had a chronic disease? When the symptoms are suppressed, you might feel good about yourself, but when the symptoms kick in, we all know how the day will be. This mood instability will make you vulnerable to depression, a serious condition that you don't want to experience. Depression can target your self-esteem, decrease your cognitive functionality, and increase your anxiety. All this might be avoided with simple exercises.

Low energy levels

From a social point of view, low energy levels caused by physical inactivity can be a serious burden. Since we are all social beings, it is in our nature to mingle with others. To go out with your friends, play with your kids or even go for a hike with your significant other, you need energy. Life is full of scenarios that require extra levels of energy. Being sedentary or just staying home and watching TV under the pretense of relaxation will kill your energy level. It becomes harder to motivate yourself to go out and explore the world.

Even at work, you need energy to focus and perform your job. As an entrepreneur, you will definitely need a lot of energy to chase your dreams. No one is going to chase them for you. Ask yourself, do I have the energy to go down that road? Because if you don't, then reconsider your position. It may not be for you, because you might either collapse along the way or just give up altogether because you lack the stamina to walk this bumpy road.

The connection between physical health and success

Now that we have an idea about the benefits of training and the risks associated with a sedentary lifestyle, there can be no doubt that there is a link between physical well-being and success. As an entrepreneur, you need to take care of yourself before you take care of others. In this ever-hectic twenty-first century, there is so much misleading information. It can affect your health directly, so it is your job to find the truth and do what is right for you and your health.

I would like to share the struggle that I went through to reverse type 2 diabetes and how I did it through research and exercise. Needless to say, I'm not a doctor or a nutritionist; I'm not qualified to tell you what to do to get the same results I did. Ultimately, you will need to do your own research and find your own ways because I believe in willpower. Where there is a will, there is always a way.

One weekend in March 2012, I was invited to a friend's house in Bahrain for breakfast. Before eating, he decided to measure his glucose level by using the sugar testing machine that many diabetic patients have at home. His sugar level was fine, and he was happy. Then he asked me if I'd had anything after I woke up, and I said no, because we were meeting for breakfast. Then he changed the needle and poked my finger to test my sugar. When he looked at my results he was shocked! I still remember his facial expression to this day.

So the breakfast suddenly turned into a trip to his doctor. Sure enough, I was diagnosed with diabetes. The whole time I was talking with the doctor, I could only hear "you can't do this, you can't eat that, you should avoid this, you shouldn't even try that." I reached a point where I had to ask if drinking water was okay. My God! All these restrictions, and then he gave me some pills that I would have to take every day for the rest of my life, to "keep it under control."

Considering that my entire family on my mother's side was diabetic and everyone on my father's side has a history of high blood pressure, I knew I would be affected at some point by at least one of the conditions. I was obese myself and physical exercise had stopped pretty much after college. My careless attitude toward these two issues came from the fact that I never really felt poorly or suffered from any of the symptoms. I thought I was okay. But that trip to the doctor is when reality started to kick in. It was like a domino effect from that point forward.

I started taking the pills, but I wasn't doing a great job at being consistent with my medication at the beginning. I felt no different with or without the pills and maybe that's why I wasn't too serious about taking them. And I wasn't the kind of person who could handle living with pills at the age of thirty-five too well. I had a hard time accepting it. I don't like pills, period. But I had no choice.

After a couple of years, I got better at taking the medication and, eventually, I got the hang of it and got my diabetes under control. Of course, that came with many food restrictions — and some cheating along the way.

Fast forward to June 18, 2014. I was in Cyprus working when I got a phone call from my mother before she went in for scheduled heart surgery. On the call, she told me that she was calling to say "goodbye." She was crying as if she knew this would the last time we spoke. I was trying to cheer her up and comfort her and tell her that she would be back in no time. After a few excruciating hours, I get a second phone call from my father saying that Mom had been admitted to the intensive care unit (ICU) and that she was unconscious. On hearing those words, panic kicked in and I immediately booked a flight to Toronto on June 21. I arrived at the Western University Hospital in London, Ontario, to see my mother's chest wide open with tubes coming out of it hooked to some biofeedback and life-support machines — a dialysis machine for the kidneys, a mechanical ventilator for the lungs, and a ventricular-assist device for the heart. The scene was nothing short of a sci-fi movie, and she remained like that in the ICU for ten days.

During those dreaded days, we were all trying to make sense of what had happened to her by asking the doctors, nurses, and even the medical students who were doing residency there. I even went to the mosque to get our imam — who happened to be a medical doctor as well — to come and visit. I thought, maybe he could get us some answers or provide some hope for us to hang on to. I wanted to know why they were using the dialysis machine and ventilator if they had operated on her heart. Why were all these machines necessary? What exactly happened in the operating theatre on that fateful day? Her organs had shut down one by one. That was all due to diabetes!

On July 2, at 12:34 p.m., the line on my mother's heart monitor went flat, shattering any hope of her coming back. The shock was immense and the pain was intolerable. I couldn't say a word because the pain in my throat made it even hard to breathe. It was so painful that I felt as if my soul was almost trying to leave my body. I couldn't take the agony of not seeing her again, at least during the rest of my life. I felt so helpless that day. It's a situation that I never wish anyone to be in.

After the funeral, I sat down by myself, grieving away from everybody, including my family. I just needed a moment to myself to rethink my position, because I had the same monster, diabetes, living inside my body and running through my veins, arteries, and capillaries. I was the only one in my family who had diabetes, so it was logical for me to think I was next. Another fact I had to consider was that all of my uncles and aunts from my mother's side had perished because of the same damn disease, diabetes! Mom was the youngest of her siblings and was the last one to go. An entire branch of the family tree from my mother's side was wiped out because of the same monster that I had. How could I think that I would be the lucky one who would live longer?

I had never understood the risk of diabetes until I saw my mother dying in front of my eyes. That's the true definition of diabetes — to watch helplessly as the disease takes life away from someone who can't help themselves, because it is too late. From that day, I was careful about my diet and about taking my medication.

Three years later, in January 2017, when I was in Cyprus, I was diagnosed with adhesive capsulitis, also known as frozen shoulder. It is a condition characterized by pain and stiffness in the shoulder joint that makes it extremely hard to move the arm. The doctor told me that it could easily be treated with minor out-patient surgery. Before the surgery, they measured my blood sugar level and told me that it was under control and that everything was okay.

On the way to the operating theatre, I was exchanging some jokes with the surgeon and the anesthesiologist just to release my tension. Before he put me under anesthesia, the latter told me that I would be out of there in about three hours. Well, that didn't happen. The three hours turned into twenty-two hours in the ICU and two more days of recovery in the hospital. After I regained consciousness in the rehabilitation room and realized that I had been unconscious for a day, I asked the doctor what happened to the three hours he had talked about. He said, "Well, with normal people it shouldn't take more than that." So I said, "What do you mean by normal people?" He said, "Non-diabetic and non-smokers — normal people!" I asked him, "So that makes me abnormal?" He replied, "I would leave that answer for you to think about, because none of the procedures or the care we are providing is considered normal under the category of frozen shoulder." "But the sugar level was okay, and you measured it before I went in," I said. He said, "True, it was normal, but you are still diabetic." Then, as I listened, he went on to explain that controlling diabetes didn't mean that you were non-diabetic. That was another wake-up call.

Even if I controlled my diabetes, my body would not respond the same way it did for non-diabetic people. I felt like I was still under the same threat of losing my life in case I had to undergo any other surgery down the line, God forbid!

Even though my diabetes was under control, I was not at all comfortable with myself. It seemed like the final decision about my life went back to diabetes — it didn't matter whether I kept it in check. That's when I made the decision to kick it out of my system completely.

After I got out of the hospital, I went to a nutritionist and my diabetes doctor to get more information about diabetes. I wanted to know everything I could about this disease. I had to deal with facts, not opinions, so I spent days and weeks researching, getting more and more inspired when I read about how you can reverse type 2 diabetes. I saw hope and I chose to latch onto it.

The first fact is that blood sugar level doesn't increase by itself. It's what I put in my mouth that causes it to surge. In other words, the problem started due to my eating habits. Another fact I learned is that being obese or overweight is a major contributor to type 2 diabetes. Why is that? Christopher Newgard, the director of the Nutrition and Metabolism Center at Duke University Medical Center, suggests that, "as you enter a state of overnutrition, as we often do living in our supersized society, all of those nutrients that come in need to be processed, stored, and utilized and the endoplasmic reticulum (ER), a factory for producing protein and the site at which blood fats (lipid) are processed, is overworked and starts sending out SOS signals. These SOS signals tell cells to dampen their insulin receptors. Insulin is the hormone that converts blood sugar to energy for the body's cells."[5] The third fact is that everyone responds to food differently. Thus, finding the right kind of food varies from one person to another. The last fact is that physical exercise is a must in all cases.

---

5   Gordon, S. "Why Does Obesity Cause Diabetes?" MedicineNet. https://www.medicinenet.com/script/main/art.asp?articlekey=39840.

An active path to health

The first step I took toward fighting diabetes was to gather all my questions and bring them to doctors and nutritionists. The conversations with doctors were almost identical. Each one recommended pills, a healthy diet, and exercise. There was always something missing in this equation. The more I read about the functionality of the pills, the more I realize that they target the symptoms, not the disease itself. So, if pills helped process the sugar in the blood, what would happen if I completely cut down my sugar intake? And why would I still need the pills if I worked out and changed my diet and made sure I didn't consume sugar? There wouldn't be any sugar overload that would require pills to be processed in the bloodstream, right?

Something didn't add up in my mind; it didn't feel right. So I started to research again, and let me tell you, the amount of information out there is enough to make you wonder and question even more. Every day, there seems to be new findings. All the chemical substances and medicines used to treat diabetes have many side effects and some of them are fatal. Pharmaceutical companies are being sued nowadays for various forms of malpractice. All these facts make it harder to believe in pills, and they make you wonder *who is benefiting from my being on pills all the time?*

One day I found some articles that talked about natural substances that can help reverse diabetes. Then I decided to go back to my doctor and talk to him about it. The articles said that there was a good chance of reversing diabetes without relying on pills if you stick to a natural diet free of carbs and sugar — and keep exercising. I wanted to know how legitimate this argument was. My doctor told me that I could use natural substances but that may not cure diabetes. Even if I controlled the sugar, I was still diabetic and those symptoms could come back if I consumed the wrong kind of food. That's why he recommended staying on the pills.

Between the articles and my doctor's opinion, things got more confusing and complicated. I still didn't understand why I needed to take pills to help process sugar if I was going to stop the sugar intake altogether. The doctor just stuck to the same line: my diabetes could recur if I didn't take care of my food and started slipping off the controlled diet and exercise. So I asked him, "Until this happens, do I need to keep my body hostage to pills? What is the wrong food? Where is the wrong in eating veggies, grilled chicken or even fish?? How exactly can this be called the wrong food?" Not getting a straight answer was a red flag.

Alternative medicine or herbal medicine

After researching more about natural substances, I visited an alternative herbal medicine clinic to talk about options for diabetes treatment. That visit was an eye-opener. The conversation with the "herbal doctor" was very different from my other consultations. He educated me about how metabolism changes as we grow older. He also mentioned that herbal medicine doesn't work the same way as its chemical counterpart. Herbal medicine is slower, but the effects last longer. In addition, herbal medicine doesn't target the symptoms, rather it focuses on the reason the body has reached a diabetic state.

Even the attitude toward diabetes was different. The herbal doctor described diabetes as a "state of being," NOT a disease. What do I mean by that? When you consume alcohol, you become drunk, which is a state of being. There is no disease called "the Drunk Disease." Similarly, when you smoke marijuana, you get stoned. Again, there is no disease called "the stoner disease." Consequently, when you consume sugar, you become diabetic. So, diabetes is NOT a disease, but rather a state of being.

Hence, to attack diabetes properly, I needed to understand what contributes to reaching this state of being diabetic, as the herbal doctor suggested. The first question the doctor asked me was, "Have you ever considered working on your metabolism in order to attack diabetes? If you fix your metabolism, then your diabetes will go away, your cholesterol level will be regulated, your blood pressure will also be normal." That's how herbal medicine works. That made a lot of sense to me and that's how I started to use some natural remedies to regulate my metabolism, and they are very effective. Substances such as cinnamon, ginger root, ginseng, cloves, turmeric, garlic, and other natural, God-created remedies are all important to regulate metabolism and enhance the immune system. Another treatment that he suggested was using Hijama — wet and dry cupping. Wet and dry cupping is an ancient practice that is still used in Middle Eastern, Persian, Chinese, and Indian cultures, among many others. Knowing that there are many alternative natural medicines and treatments out there gave me hope and made my will stronger.

The nutritionist

My next stop was the nutritionist. That's when I got to learn about those fancy diet programs that have support groups, mobile applications, calorie charts, calorie calculators, and all that jazz. I learned what good and bad carbs are, what good and bad fats are, protein, sugar ... etc. Then I got to learn how to calculate my calories and how to choose my food. All this made the situation more complicated and frustrating for me. I told my nutritionist that there was no way on earth I could follow those kinds of diets. I was not going to count calories; I was not going to a support group for my eating habits. I just needed the facts and I would tailor my life the way it would serve me best.

Understanding food

Understanding food is a basic necessity for any diabetic person. I encourage everyone who is diabetic to see a dietitian. A lot of the food on supermarket shelves is simply not healthy. The food industry is also another enemy of the diabetic. There is no healthy food that doesn't expire for months or a couple of years; they have chemicals that work as preservatives, which can have side effects on your body. Bottom line, if it doesn't grow on trees and shrubs, or in the ground, then you shouldn't eat it. Anything that goes through a process is not good for you. Ready-to-eat meals are not healthy, packaged food is not healthy, sugar-loaded desserts are not healthy, all kinds of carbonated drinks, including power drinks, are not healthy, all sugar-free or fat-free food is not healthy, all sugar substitutes are not healthy.

Anything white is not good for you. White sugar, flour and salt — they are all processed. Either consume them in their natural state or avoid them altogether. It doesn't make any sense to go looking for a substitute for something that is not good for you to begin with. For example, sugar is highly addictive, so why would anyone go looking for substitutes for something that is dangerous for your health? It is like looking for a "health-friendly" version of cocaine. The point is to quit sugar, not find a substitute for it.

Thinking about all this, I came to the conclusion that our current eating habits are not normal. This is why we get all these diseases. If the food we eat is not healthy, why should we expect healthy results? It doesn't make sense. The best way is to buy natural ingredients and cook them yourself at home. Instead of trying to convince yourself that processed food is healthy, think about the facts. For example, people run to buy stevia products thinking they are healthy. Well, stevia leaves are green in nature, so why is the stevia powder white?? If I want to grind the leaves myself, then I should end up with green powder or paste. Think about that and ponder how healthy it is. Do the homework yourself. No one is going to do it for you.

Last stop — the gym

My last stop was the gym. I signed up with a personal trainer who could help me on my weight-loss journey. With a toned, defined body and lean muscles, he was definitely qualified to advise me on how to work out and how to eat. Understanding more about food from the dietitian had made quite a difference in the way I looked at eating and exercise.

Once I had explained my condition to my trainer, he was able to work with me and suggest a dietary plan and workout programs. He also asked me to check with my doctor and dietitian to ensure the plan was okay, and I did. After I got the green light, I began working on losing weight, eating healthy. That year, I took three HbA1c tests to measure the history of glucose in my blood and the results were between 4.5–5 mmol/L, which meant that I was in the non-diabetic zone. It was also important that I measured my blood sugar levels before, during, and after training. I had to observe how my food habits and the workout program worked hand in hand to get a better understanding of what I should do and what I should avoid. It took me some time to get a grip on my health but eventually all the hard work and determination paid off. This is how I managed to reverse my diabetes.

Again, I'm neither a doctor, an alternative medicine expert, a nutritionist, nor a gym trainer. But I did manage to reverse the status of my diabetes using personal research as my starting place. I strongly encourage diabetic people to educate themselves about their personal scenarios and do whatever it takes to get themselves out of their situation. Find *your* ways, do your own research, go talk to many doctors, find the truth, but don't surrender to this fate. It is reversible in many cases, more so in type 2 than type 1. No matter what, don't give up.

There is no doubt that changing one's lifestyle requires a great deal of effort — especially when it feels like everything around us is not healthy. Sometimes, we even create our own hurdles to avoid a healthy lifestyle. Making the change requires effort, conviction, and determination.

Let me share with you some of the obstacles that I created for myself just to resist exercising. The first excuse had to do with my commitment to the gym. Since I travel a lot for work, I was trying to convince myself that I wouldn't know what to do if I went to a gym without my trainer. But the reality is that most of the exercises I needed to do — be it walking, jogging, or swimming — didn't require a gym or a trainer. All I had to do was put in at least a hundred and fifty minutes of moderate aerobic exercise in a week, or seventy-five minutes of vigorous aerobic exercise.

The other excuse I made was money. It is expensive to have a personal trainer and pay for gym membership fees. But you can find many workout routines online that don't require a personal trainer or a gym membership. Most aerobic activities and strength training, such as squats, push-ups, sit-ups, or running, rely only on your own body weight. You can also lift weights at home or use a chair to help with your leg exercises. You can join a gym with minimal membership fees. You can also ask a friend who knows about workout programs to help you get going. Leading a healthy life requires physical activity, not a gym membership. A gym is a nice bonus for sure, but not a requirement.

Another thing that frustrated me when I thought about changing my eating habits was the deprivation of all the foods that I loved and how I would have to spend my life without them. Well, here's the thing! Once you exercise and have control over your health and food, you will be allowed to cheat now and then, and enjoy that flavor you've been craving so badly. The point here is that you are the one who is supposed to be in control, not food. Once you get into the routine of eating healthy, it will become second nature. You won't feel the deprivation because, in reality, you are not deprived of anything. You are shifting the decision-making process from your stomach to your brain. That's the effect of training and eating healthy, and you will enjoy it for the rest of your life.

Now that I have explained what my physical life looks like, I would like you to start working on yours. If you are already exercising, then keep it up. But if you are not, then there is some homework for you to do. First, I want you to educate yourself more about the food industry and the pharmaceutical industry so you can understand how they both work and what kind of supplements you may need along the way. Compare the nutritional values of regular fruits and vegetables and processed fruits and vegetables. Read more about fat-free or sugar-free food and find out why they are not healthy. In this era, it is important that you understand what you eat, otherwise it is your health that will suffer the consequences.

Second, I want you to allocate some time to exercise. Start with walking to get into the habit of getting out of your house for some physical activity. Try not to sit down for a long period of time. When you go to the supermarket for grocery shopping, walk down all the aisles without exceptions. You can walk around the store twice if you want. Call a friend and suggest going for a hike somewhere. Whatever you do, don't be idle.

My last recommendation is to have a complete medical check-up just to understand where you stand from a health perspective. Remember, as we grow older, our bodies change and slow down. Find out what's happening with your body — how it is changing and where it is heading. Nothing stays the same on this earth, including your own body. So, it is important to spot the weaknesses now, instead of paying for them down the line. We only live once, so make sure you live healthy.

And remember, as a future entrepreneur, you will need your body to be healthy and strong because it is the vehicle that you will use to spread your impact on this world. It is not going to be easy, so prepare your body to handle it now.

6
The Power of the Mind

Read.

— Holy Qur'an (96:1)

THE BRAIN IS the center of intelligence through which one understands the world and how it works. It is also a place where ideas are born and are manifested. It is important to understand that all the beautiful things that have been done on this earth, as well as all the horrible things, started with an idea or an expression born in the mind. Once an idea starts to grow in the mind, the brain automatically works on executing it in many forms.

The soul gives you purpose; the heart gives you values and principles that motivate your purpose; your body becomes the place that your soul calls home; and the brain gives you the power to manifest your thoughts into a living reality.

This powerful organ can be used or abused, depending on what your purpose is. The brain is so powerful that it is unstoppable if you believe in your ideas or expressions. You can start a war or a charitable organization. You can be a demon or a human being, simply by putting that thought into your head. History can give you many examples of how people have used or abused their minds to reach the place they chose to be. Mahatma Gandhi became Gandhi with the ideas he believed in; Adolf Hitler became Hitler through the same mechanism — an idea in the brain that shaped his personality and dictated his behavior.

The power of the mind

Of all the powers we have talked about, the power of the mind is the trickiest. It is a lot easier to find your purpose than find ways to fulfill it. This is simply because you will spend more time — maybe your whole life — in the trial-and-error stage than in any other.

It is easier to believe in the benefits of universal values like love, compassion, honesty, and integrity than to find ways to embrace them and execute them on a daily basis. You need your brain for execution, but first a process of thinking has to take place to find those ways. For example, when I found my purpose in life — educating people — I went through a whole process of thinking about how exactly I was going to do it. Thoughts about my lack of a degree in education and not knowing how to teach were combating my self-confidence. This sort of mental struggle is normal; I expected it to happen, because that's a natural product of the thinking process. My brain was learning new ways of thinking because what I was going through was new territory for me. Slowly I started to find my way, even to the point of writing this book. I don't need a degree in education to share my experience with people. Each of us is capable of teaching or leading by example.

It was my brain that held me back, by believing in self-created false ideas, and it was the same brain that freed me of this scenario once I forced it to think differently. It is very important to create the right thoughts in our minds and find ways to develop those positive thoughts so they can grow and force our behavior and character to accompany them.

So let's talk about how impactful the brain is and how it can help shape your new character.

Benefits of brainpower
Intellectual expansion

To begin with, you should understand that mental power is capable of expanding your horizons. While there are many ways to sharpen mental power, researchers have found that reading is the superfood for the brain. The more you read and educate yourself, the more you will learn about life. Reading a book can take you places without leaving your chair. You will be exposed to different cultures, languages, schools of thoughts, to new business practices and new technological development ... you name it. As Dr. Seuss said, "The more that you read, the more things you will know. The more that you learn, the more places you will go."

They say that the fastest and least expensive trip is to read a book. Through reading, one can have great opportunities to understand other people's perspectives about life and how they process it. It can help develop learning methods about other cultures that might be beneficial to entrepreneurship. Since we all think and perceive life differently, our needs and demands are different as well. Every nation, culture, or subculture has its own way of doing things. Understanding those ways can make it easier for the entrepreneur to penetrate those markets.

More educated decisions

Since the brain is the center of intelligence and the powerhouse where decision-making happens, increasing your knowledge can help you make better-informed decisions and have better judgment on more complex issues in your life. Ohio State University researchers found that reading about someone who overcame obstacles can motivate you to meet your own goals and objectives. Say, for example, you start to read about a character who overcomes poverty and reaches success after consistent hard work. After becoming familiar with the character's situation, the emotions they went through, and the road they took, you begin to get motivated to do the same. The more you identify with that character, their experience, and their circumstances — as if they were also happening to you — the more likely you will be to take action. Intellectual well-being is crucial to improving critical thinking skills that will help develop other problem-solving and coping skills, which are vital to staying intelligent and productive.

Enriching social relationships

Not only can an enhanced intellectual state help you make better decisions, but it can also help enrich social relationships. David Comer Kidd and Emanuele Castano suggest in research published in *Science* that "understanding others' mental state is a crucial skill that enables the complex social relationships that characterize human societies."

When you immerse yourself deep enough in a good read, you get to understand how others think, and it connects you to their feelings, making you more empathetic. It is important to master this emotional connection between people since we don't live alone on this planet and we need to accommodate each other. For us to do that, we need to understand each other and learn how to coexist.

Increase in cognitive abilities

Another interesting piece of research, done at the University of Santiago de Compostela in Spain, shows that having a rich vocabulary can significantly delay the manifestation of mental decline. When the researchers analyzed vocabulary tests scores for more than three hundred volunteers who were fifty and older, they concluded that participants with lower scores were three to four times more vulnerable to the risk of cognitive decay than participants with the highest scores. A large vocabulary promotes a more resilient mind by fueling what scientists call "cognitive reserve." Cognitive reserve can be described as your brain's ability to cope with damages. It helps the brain find different mental pathways around areas that have been damaged by stroke, dementia, or any other form of decay, and create new connections. Research suggests that learning another language or a new musical instrument is one of the best things you can do at any age. People who speak multiple languages (polyglots) have been shown to be stronger at multitasking and superior at memorizing; they have the ability to focus more than their monolingual counterparts. Dr. Thomas Bak of the University of Edinburgh suggests that a brain that learns a second language early in life will likely see more cognitive advantages than a late-life learner. He also says that "just having the basics of those linguistic connections can delay dementia." It is never too late to open a book and learn something new.

As human beings, we are either moving forward or going backward; we are never stagnant. If you are not moving forward, then you are definitely falling back. In his book *The 7 Habits of Highly Effective People*, Stephen Covey said, "TV is on in most homes some 35–45 hours a week. That's as much as many people put in their jobs, more than most put into school." There are many distractions around us that can seem more important than developing our lives. Many people don't realize the dangerous consequences of time wasting, especially when it comes to wasting it in front of the TV. When you watch TV, you are subconsciously subscribing to the values that are being broadcasted through that tube. At the very least, you are entertaining those values more than paying attention to yours, let alone empowering them.

What happens when you neglect the power of the brain?

Loss of purpose

Finding your purpose requires mental work and education about yourself or the path you need to follow, so being reluctant to go that route means lost opportunities for achieving your purpose. An aimless life without purpose or interest is less valuable than a tree's, since the tree has a purpose and is living its life to fulfill it. The Buddha once said, "The mind is everything; what you think you become." If your mind is busy with nothing, then what will you become? Nothing, I guess!

Becoming stagnant

If you neglect the power of your brain, you will not only lose your sense of purpose but also lose opportunities for self-development and growth. The only way to get out of stagnation is to move forward and push yourself further, because the brain doesn't develop by itself. It needs to exercise as well, and since you can't exercise mental muscles at the gym, you need to read and learn. That's how the brain grows. If you don't give it materials to think about, to process, to learn from, then it will stay where it is. What kind of life do you think you will have if your brain stops growing? Reflect on that for a minute.

Obsolete knowledge

Another drawback of neglecting brain power — especially these days, when technology is advancing every minute — is that current knowledge goes obsolete at a much faster rate than before. If you don't catch up with life, then life will pass you by, and it is not going to wait for you to catch up. Education doesn't stop at university degrees. Reading, taking classes, learning new things are all forms of education. Constant education is necessary because you can't rely on one source for education all the time.

There is a solid relationship between the power of the mind and exponential growth and success. Just like you need to empower your body and enrich your soul, you also need to expand your brain if you are sincere about developing yourself.

My learning journey

Reading is something that I do daily, even if it is only one page. I developed this habit when I started 3mushrooms in Bahrain and felt that my knowledge was getting outdated. To give a little more background to the story here, I graduated from university in 1999 and started 3mushrooms in 2012. In those thirteen years, life shifted dramatically and very quickly. Business was being conducted in ways I had never thought about when I was in college. Social media, for example, was nonexistent back then. Similarly, marketing had evolved, because the ways we reached our potential customers were very different. Traditional marketing tools like TV or direct mail were no longer as effective as they used to be. New business concepts had appeared. New consumer behavior had surfaced. New ways of customer interaction had been introduced.

To be successful, I felt the need to do whatever it took to get back in the game and find my way through all of this. My knowledge from university was either inadequate or outdated. So I registered for professional development classes at the Cyprus International Institute of Management (CIIM), both to refresh and upgrade my knowledge and to get in touch with the ways of a younger generation. I needed to understand their mentality, the way they interacted with each other and with the world and their attitude to the world around them. I also wanted to discover what kind of changes were happening in the business environment. It was like a complete overhaul. and it felt like schooling was never going to end.

Old versus new
While in school, it was important for me to connect with my professors to discuss how business had shifted and how new practices have been adopted. I began with the evolution of the marketing tools used to promote businesses. Back in the '90s, print media like newspapers and direct mail were in circulation all the time. Trade magazines were the best tools to reach consumers and build brand awareness. The Yellow Pages was another marketing tool. Big printed ads used to attract more consumers because they gave a perception of how big the business was. It was the same case with billboards, TV slots, and fax advertisements, because marketing budgets were very high back then.

Marketing has taken a new role and a new shape. It has become more of a science than a communication tool. Today, it's all about data science; our lives have transformed to the digital platform and everything is governed by algorithms and speculations. New concepts have emerged, such as Search Engine Optimization (SEO) and Search Engine Marketing (SEM) over the web, among other new digital marketing languages such as Pay Per

Click marketing. People now talk about influencers — a person with the ability to influence potential buyers of a product or service by promoting or recommending the items on social media — as a marketing tool. They use tracking analytics and data interpreters to speculate behavior or target advertising. Marketing has become a new animal altogether. The need to understand all these changes and educate myself about the new meaning of marketing was vital. I had to adapt and evolve. In addition to learning about business practices, I also took social media marketing classes at the same institute to make sure that I was up-to-date and would feel more confident and clearer about my path.

The search for knowledge continues

When I look back at 2012, the only thing I had was the network, not the cash and not the know-how, and I needed to have all three. Since know-how is much easier to get than cash, I decided to read more about satellite communications, attend seminars about the topic, talk to suppliers, visit the library, research the internet, and talk to people on LinkedIn.

I still read about the subject to educate myself further; it is a constantly evolving technology. I need to be on top of technological advances in the maritime satellite communication sector. With new advancements come new features, benefits, and values. It is extremely important to understand all this so I can sell the technology. Meanwhile, it was also important to educate myself about the terrestrial internet so I could draw comparisons between it and the internet at sea. I had to read more and more to gain the expertise to explain the huge difference in costs for getting a connection on these surfaces.

I guess life would have been easier if I were a computer science graduate or a network engineer or a communication engineer, but I'm not. I'm a business graduate; to get a grip on my line of work, I had to read and get a mentor to show me the way. It can be difficult, for sure, but it is never impossible. It does require a lot of work and a lot of time and effort, but the results are worth all those efforts.

Read, educate, and close deals

As an entrepreneur, it is natural to pay attention to all aspects of your business and spend a lot of time thinking and working on developing it further. I observed that with a high level of energy and harmony was established the minute I start educating my clients about the technology they were subscribing to in our meetings. I have also noticed a difference in response when I try to sell the product and/or the service as opposed to selling their *benefits* and *values*. The latter is a much more effective selling technique. People respond much more positively when they understand the value of the product or the service I want to sell them. It provides a clearer picture and a better answer for the "what's in it for me?" question. Once clients spot the values that this product or service will bring them, closing the deal is pretty much a piece of cake.

I decided to hold workshops for my clients, to educate them about our technology, about what's out there in the market, about what is going to be abandoned soon, about what is worth investing in, about what technologies are currently replaceable, and about how all this can affect their operations and finances. The results were very powerful. These seminars helped establish trust simply through education. They also paved the way toward clients' loyalty, positioned 3mushrooms as a leader in the market, and offered a source of client empowerment, through knowledge. 3mushrooms is a leading brand in the Arabian Gulf region in the satellite communications industry. All this started with reading.

My first workshop

Before I started my first event, I was clueless. I didn't know the technicalities of hosting an event, how to get sponsors, how to market it, how to structure it, get attendees, get hotel packages for my clients coming from overseas, and so on. I wondered how I could handle all these expenses and how they would reflect on 3mushrooms' revenue. What did I need to do? I educated myself about event hosting. Once again, it was back to the internet and research, consulting friends in the entertainment industry, getting in touch with the marketing department of my suppliers and asking for their cooperation. I approached social media marketing companies to find out how they could help advertise the event. All this was because I wanted to be better at educating my customer and I wanted to create a difference in the region. That's the core value of 3mushrooms and its Unique Value Proposition — Learn, save, and enjoy a reliable and fast connection at sea.

Leadership through education

Reading is like stepping into an ocean of knowledge. It forces your mind to wander and enquire. It opens many doors that may not currently be obvious to you. You can't read about different business aspects without stumbling across the topic of leadership. The current trend of leadership is vastly different from what it was back in 1999.

I started thinking about new leadership styles; I wanted to know if there was a "science" behind it or a way to make it better. Once again, I started reading more, I went back to professors and asked more questions, I read some business case studies they recommended; I kept all my options open and available when needed. At this point, I was very happy to be the absorbing sponge, seeking knowledge anywhere I went. I had to let my creativity flow and experiment with my ideas to test them and validate them.

The application of 3mushrooms' philosophy

To truly adopt the 3mushrooms' business philosophy of co-growth, I had to look internally and seek opportunities for development. The best opportunity was in the most valuable asset that 3mushrooms has — its team members. Since our 3mushrooms family is diverse and its team members come from different backgrounds (American, Cypriot, Armenian, Greek, Italian, Indian, Sri Lankan), I needed to spread the one-family concept with mutually agreed values that would create our own new identities as "mushrooms."

What is the value that 3mushrooms can bring to its team-mates? Co-growth! As a family, we grow together, just like mushrooms do, without leaving anyone behind. Our clients, our vendors, our suppliers, our teammates, and our investors will grow together; that's the 3mushrooms effect that I want to establish. So how do I do that internally? Simply by providing value to my family members. Realizing that our collective growth would not happen by itself, I had to embrace our philosophy of co-growth, and I had to develop my leadership style.

So, I asked myself, "What kind of a leader do I want to be?" By reflecting on what had worked with my clients in my past experiences, I decided to be consistent and apply the same method internally. That's when the topic of coaching overtook my heart and I started to enjoy being ON PURPOSE! Leadership requires extending one's self to be of service to others. To know how to deal with others, motivate them, and push them forward requires skills that I needed to develop. That's why coaching was the answer to my question about the type of leader I wanted to be. It is still compatible with my values.

My self-limiting beliefs

As beautiful as all this might sound to you, it is important to realize that it doesn't come easily, especially at the beginning. There were many limiting beliefs and self-created doubts that pulled me back to my comfort zone; they kept me from exploring foreign territories and expanding my brain power. My brain resisted change. There were moments when I felt scared — of failure, of embarrassment, and getting stuck in the "what if?" limbo. But today, looking back, I realize that challenging those thoughts was the best thing I have ever done in my life. I learned to say enough is enough. To take charge of my life and lead it the way I want to. To choose to happen to life as opposed to letting life happen to me.

Was it difficult? Of course! Worth it? Every single moment of it. Would I do it again? ABSOLUTELY, in a New York minute!

Now, let me share some of the limiting beliefs that I used to surrender to. The first thought was that I needed money to continue my education to reach my goals. Well, the truth is that degrees are not required to pursue knowledge. There is a difference in purpose between seeking a degree and seeking knowledge. Some people choose to go after degrees to acquire status — social, academic, career, or any other kind of status. Degrees do not guarantee success. They only show the specific status that the person is seeking. Mark Zuckerberg, the co-founder of Facebook, is a Harvard dropout. He sacrificed his degree to pursue success.

What matters here is having knowledge and doing something with it, not simply having knowledge to store in your head. Success requires a balance between knowing and doing. This truth has made me thirsty for knowledge about the things I want to put into use. So I bought some books and started to read. Just getting started gave me a stronger sense of hope for a better future, a stronger will, and a refreshing, positive energy. The first word that was revealed in the Qur'an, "Read," flashed in my thoughts, as if it were a confirmation from my spiritual domain that reading is essential and a crucial part of growth. That belief was a confirmation that I was onto something. I was on a mission to seek and execute: seek knowledge and put it into practice.

The other challenge that I had to go through was what I call the universal "I don't have time" excuse. I used to find it frustrating to pick up a book and read it because it requires time and dedication. It felt like another unwanted "job," and because of that feeling, reading wasn't high on my priority list. I find it interesting that people use the phrase "I don't have time" casually. What they are actually saying is, "It's not important to me and doesn't have a priority on my list." We all find the time when we decide to do things and let our creativity loose to find all possible ways to achieve our objectives.

We humans try our best to find the time for important things in our lives. For example, when we decide to take care of our health and change our lifestyle, we find the time to go to the gym, because we realize how important it is in our journey toward a healthier life. Another example is watching TV shows. Not only do some people find the time to watch them, but they also have the dedication to watch all the seasons, with great anticipation for new ones to come. Why? Because entertainment has importance for them.

On the other hand, if a certain activity or a decision is not relevant to our interest, we tend to focus on its negative aspects. Let's use the gym example again. If health is not high on someone's priority list, then going to the gym might prove to be a bit difficult. While they may not deny the importance of working out, they are not going to find the time for it. They find themselves focusing on the negatives about working out, like sweating and feeling fatigued because the muscles ache the next day, and so forth. It is easier to say, "I don't have time," when in reality, they would have the time if taking care of their health was high on their list.

It is all about having the interest to make the decisions and take the actions required to achieve the goal. Reading, educating yourself, and even challenging your mental abilities are extremely important, and once you realize their importance and establish an interest, then you will find the time for them.

The other obstacle that I had to go through was challenging my talent for sleeping when it came to reading. I can fall asleep in no time — often by the time I finish the third page or so. Not to mention that my reading speed is slightly below "adequate." I find it hard not to get sidetracked by my thoughts or shift my focus while trying to visualize the scenario I'm reading. I get lost in details, trying to complete the picture rather than pay attention to the point the author is trying to make. Sometimes, after a few pages, my eyes continue to read, but I realize that my mind has already smoothly drifted away, to a phone call that I have to make or a task I need to finish, or whatever. Then I have to go back and read from the beginning of the page so that I don't miss anything. Keeping my focus on reading was really challenging at first and even frustrating. I used to wonder how some people found it relaxing!

Thanks to technology, we now have access to audiobooks across many mobile devices. It works well for me. It is a lot easier for me to listen to a book than read it and have to fight falling asleep. I don't get sidetracked as often anymore. I'm more focused, as if I'm present in a conversation and I'm just listening. I also finish more books in less time. Since I travel often, audiobooks are an additional advantage. I can listen to them over my headphones on planes and in airports where it might be difficult to concentrate on a book. I find it beneficial to buy both the book and the audio version of things I have real interest in, so I can listen and read with my eyes as well. I really enjoy the results of this technique. There is something about touching the pages in a book and flipping it that reassures you that you can come back to passages as needed. It beats lots of rewinding and forwarding until you get to that specific piece you want to listen to again. So, as I said earlier, there are many different ways to read a book. Education is always available everywhere around you. There is always a solution to every challenge. You just need to establish an interest in it.

Enhancing the power of the mind

What can you do to start working on enhancing your mental power? Before anything, you need to realize that knowledge is a key factor for success. You need to keep the brain active and the best thing you can do is to keep learning. I want you to find a subject that is truly relevant to your interest and read more about it. Sign up for newsletters and research it on the internet. Find discussion groups around that topic and get engaged in meaningful discussions or debates. Discuss it with your friends.

If you can, sign up for classes, either online or in a local institute. This will be very effective, because you will meet people with similar interests to talk to and learn from. It is also a great way to engage yourself with that professional community, allowing you to ask your questions and listen to different opinions, or even different ways of thinking. Just keep acquiring knowledge every day and dedicate some time in your daily schedule for reading.

Another thing that you can do to stretch your mental muscles is doing mental activity challenges such as puzzles, chess, writing for pleasure, drawing, painting, or even learning a new language. Knowledge doesn't necessarily mean that you have to read about a specific subject or topic. Expand your horizon and become a person of knowledge. Don't restrict yourself to certain areas. You can also watch channels like the Discovery Channel, National Geographic, Animal Planet, History Channel, or anything educational and fun to watch. Strengthening your mental power can be very entertaining. It doesn't have to come through institutions and certifications. The most important thing is to keep your mind challenged and active.

Also, remember that exercising and meditation are very important. As kids, we learned that a great mind is in a great body. So physical health is closely related to your mental health. Try to exercise daily; keep your body active to enrich your blood circulation so your brain can have its share as well.

This domain is the one that requires a lot of determination, commitment, and flexibility. Acquiring knowledge must be a part of you if you decide to become an entrepreneur. Entering the world of entrepreneurship without being ready will cost you a lot of money. Make sure you know how to swim before you jump into the entrepreneurship ocean. You don't have to be a perfect swimmer. But at least have some knowledge and the necessary basics that will allow you to jump, swim, and learn more skills while swimming. So be prepared to read as much as you can and educate yourself about your purpose, your journey, and how to achieve your goals. Entrepreneurship can be a suicidal path if walked with an idle mind.

7
Become the Future You

The wise adapt themselves to circumstances,
as water molds itself to the pitcher.

— *Chinese Proverb*

NOW THAT WE have discovered the powers that consti-
tute a human being, we need to start capitalizing on those
powers to create the new SUPER YOU, the one who will
lead a successful and meaningful life. Developing oneself
requires embracing new qualities and getting rid of the ones
that never helped you. Before we jump into entrepreneurship, it is important to understand that entrepreneurship
starts with you as a person as opposed to your business. It
is YOU who will be an entrepreneur, not your business. The
business that you will create is only a consequence of the
decisions resulting from your entrepreneurial spirit. Also,
just like any profession, there are some skills and qualities

necessary to fulfilling your role in that position. If you were a member of a basketball team, you would probably need to have an athletic body, good stamina, the ability to dribble the ball and jump and shoot, the ability to be a team player. You can't be obese and expect to be drafted into the National Basketball Association.

Being an entrepreneur also requires special skills and knowledge. While some people are natural leaders or natural entrepreneurs, you need to know that anyone can develop these skills and acquire the necessary knowledge to become successful. Entrepreneurship is a lot of hard work, a lot of sleepless nights, and a lot of hours every day, but it is not impossible. The minute you understand your purpose and start your entrepreneurial journey, learning will become your lifelong mission and reading will become your best hobby. You also need to realize that you have to transform, and you have to embrace change. You have to be open to the idea of evolving and adapting. You need to acquire all the skills that will allow this smooth transition in your life to happen. The more flexible you are, the easier life will become. You just need to keep the word "CHANGE" in your mind and make it a part of your DNA.

Life is constantly changing
Why do we need to embrace change? Simply because nothing stays the same on this earth. The world is constantly evolving. The world's economic powers are

shifting, the way we do business does not remain static, the educational system has moved to online platforms. Even the way we socialize is different.

If everything is changing, why shouldn't you? We — humans — cannot afford to lead a stagnant life. We have to cope with life to be able to live it comfortably, instead of racing it or trying to fight it.

Adaptability

A major difference between the unsuccessful and the successful individual is the latter's willingness to challenge their comfort zone by continuous learning and adapting to their ever-evolving surroundings. Adaptability is a competitive advantage; it will add value to your thinking. For example, employers are always on the lookout for people who have the right attitude, who accept change and demonstrate adaptability. They look for them because it is a sign of effective leadership. Such people know how to take advantage of any circumstances or situation because they are willing to adjust their ways. Adaptability will also help you become happier and more satisfied.

Guy Winch, a psychologist, once said, "We constantly meet psychological challenges. Some of us succumb, we feel hopeless, disempowered, give up ... and some meet challenges, take the knock and learn something from it. Our ability to have life satisfaction, to be happy [and] to have good relationships really depends on our ability to adapt." Moreover, adaptability is important for improved mental health. Being adaptable will help you bounce back very quickly from adversity. Bad things can happen, but when you are adaptable, you adjust your thoughts and expectations based on your new reality, rather than dwell on the negative outcome. It is a lot easier to tweak your attitude to adapt to your circumstances than it is to change your circumstances.

Who do you want to be?

Change also becomes the path that will lead to the best version of yourself. If you feel there is more you can do in life, yet you are not doing it, then something needs to change. Think about it, if whatever you have been doing hasn't been helping you to reach your destination, then modifying the old ways becomes very important. If we don't alter our ways, then we shouldn't expect different outcomes, right?

Once you are clear about the person you want to be in the future, you will find yourself correcting your way of thinking, your habits, and even your behavior to become that new person — the new leader. You won't be able to reach your goal if you decide to stay where you are now and continue with what you are doing today. You will grow through the challenges that change brings. The more you challenge yourself, the more creative and powerful you become. The leader within you won't come out until you modify your current ways of thinking and doing. Then your soul will summon your inner hero to execute your purpose and objectives. Will you allow this to happen?

Plan your journey

Not only is change important for your new character, but it also goes hand in hand with planning the future. When you sit down to plan your life, you get to think about the things that matter to you the most. You will be able to see what exactly you want out of life. You will be able to understand your goals without any confusion. It will show you the kind of life that you want to have and your desired destination. In addition, planning will also give you the tools to measure how far you have come — and how much further it is to your destination. Planning will help you avoid tasks or activities that waste your time and delay reaching your goals.

Creating a plan also gives you control — *you* will be the one making decisions and considering different options. And when you do that, your plan becomes more attainable to you. It no longer looks or feels so far from reality. Moreover, planning your life will teach you how to say "NO" to activities, tasks, or anything that takes you from your dream or does not help you reach it. The best part about planning is how powerful it will make you feel — because you will be planning a life you have always desired. You'll feel more passionate about life and eager to live it to the fullest.

Invest your time

Of course, for all this to happen, you need to invest your time wisely. Embracing the new you will help give you control over your time. If you think about it, we all have two selves. One lives in the present and is usually consumed by life's current circumstances, and the other lives in the future and is probably adding the finishing touches on the retirement home. We mostly invest in our future wants and needs, but some of our investment needs to be in the present time, to help build the new character that will live in the future.

Our present selves are mostly disconnected from our future selves. We don't pay attention to time the way we pay attention to other resources like water or electricity. We are all keen to turn the water or electricity off when we are not using them, correct? We try to conserve because we value those resources. But we treat time as if we have an unlimited supply of it. Every second that passes cannot be replaced, yet we spend it frivolously, sometimes we even say we are "killing time."

What should you invest your time in? Well, sleep for one. Yes, sleep! Sleep is as important as food and water for a quality life. Make sure you give your body the rest it deserves. Invest in your health and support it. Invest time in planning your day or your life. Invest time in self-development. Brian Tracey said, "If you wish to achieve worthwhile things in your personal and career life, you must become a worthwhile person in your own self-development." Invest in your family and relationships. Invest in new hobbies to expand your horizons. As long as you are doing something that has a positive impact and will help you down the line, then invest some time in it.

It is very important that you adopt the philosophy of change to become who you want to be. Doing things without believing in the outcome is futile. It is the willingness to adapt that will make you harvest all the benefits that transformation can bring. In his book *What's the Future of Business?* Brian Solis mentions an interesting statistic that shows the power of change. He said that "over 40% of the companies that were at the top of the *Fortune* 500 in 2000 were no longer there in 2010." Transformation is a reality; it is constantly happening and denying it can only lead to failure. You must adapt; you must evolve.

Not achieving your purpose

How would it feel living a life where you can't achieve your purpose because you are not willing to rethink your ways? Change can open up many doors and possibilities for you to reach your purpose. Without change, there is confusion. Confusion happens when there is nothing new for you to try and there is nothing different coming into your life. You miss out on meeting interesting people, enjoying an adventurous experience, learning top-notch skills, entertaining fresh ideas, or learning alternative techniques that will elevate you and make your purpose clearer.

Good but not great

You also lose the chance of becoming great. It is easy to stay in the comfort zone when you feel "good"; you will stay there as long as being good is "good enough." You miss out on all the potential opportunities of becoming even greater when you are not flexible. Many of us don't know what we are missing out on because we have never extended ourselves to explore those opportunities. Lack of adaptability and resistance to change make it easier for us to stay in our comfort zone and stop progressing. Jim Collins, a prominent figure in the area of business management and company sustainability and growth, said, "Good is the enemy of great. And that is one of the key reasons why we have so little that becomes great. We don't have great schools, principally because we have good schools. We don't have great government, principally because we have good government. Few people attain great lives, in large part because it is just so easy to settle for a good life."

Being reactive

Another disadvantage to not being flexible is that you become reactive instead of proactive. When you accept and seek change, you take control over your life; decisions are made from the consciousness of the need to adapt. This puts the direction of your life in your own hands. Choosing to stay the same is similar to choosing to be a victim controlled by outside forces. Tweaking your character requires proactivity, and proactivity also demands flexibility. When you accept change, coping with life will be a lot easier.

Fewer flavors

Change can introduce new flavors to life. Many stories, books, or movies are about how regular people go through transformation and become heroes. In every good legend, there is a hard start and a liberating end. That's what naturally attracts us — human beings in human stories. If there is no alteration that the main character has to undertake, then there is no story. The character becomes boring and perhaps unlikeable.

The changes that occur during the journey are what make life interesting and unique. The more experiences we have, the more we learn, the more we achieve. Denying yourself the permission to evolve is like denying what life has to offer you. Life is less exciting when you stay the same. What story do you want to tell the world? What adjustments need to happen today to create that hero you want to be in the future?

Moreover, when you decide to push yourself outside your comfort zone, your mind will be stretched and you will start acquiring new knowledge, new perspectives on life, and new ways to enjoy it. Creating self-limiting beliefs such as "I need formal education and the degree to back it up in order to succeed" can foster an environment that resists change. The reason why such limiting thoughts dictate people's lives is that they are never challenged or tested and validated. If you accept staying where you are and not moving forward, there won't be anything for you to learn anymore. You also deny the chance to learn about yourself. You don't get the opportunity to actually prove to yourself that you are who you think you are. It takes a lot of adaptability to develop new ideas, better skills, and a fresh outlook on life. Change is the key to a brighter future. Don't deny yourself that chance.

Take action

Now that we have come this far, it is time for you to start taking action and ignite your transformation. We have talked about many aspects of life that need attention to achieve balance and help you become the super you. Let's start your journey together. Let's start getting a better understanding of the exciting character you will be creating. There will be a lot of exploring, a lot of positive emotions, and some negative emotions as well. We will be stepping into foreign territories, becoming curious about them together. Embrace your journey and all the values that it will bring you. Welcome the change with your arms wide open. Bring your dedication and focus with you throughout this journey. Be true to your-self and believe in yourself.

Our first step will be about discovering passion and purpose. It is important to understand that you might have more than one passion. You may also have multiple purposes. For example, you can be an inventor and an educator at the same time, two different purposes that complement each other. Or you could have passions for cooking and flying. Everything is possible. What is important is to realize them and determine the actions needed to empower them or make a business out of them. So, how do we start?

I would like you to print the exercises below, grab a pen, and go to a place where you can connect with nature, a park, a beach, a desert, a forest. In such places, people tend to be more calm, creative, and comfortable. What matters is for you to be in a peaceful environment and pay undivided attention to yourself. This is "YOUR TIME," so make sure nothing will distract you. You will spend some time reflecting on your life and asking yourself some ques-tions. Make sure you write down your answers, because it is very important for you to see what your thoughts are. Seeing what you think in front of your eyes (as opposed to leaving them locked in your brain) makes it easier for you to have control over your thoughts; they are exposed now. So make sure you write down every feeling you experience and any thought that passes through your mind while you are doing these exercises.

Exercise 1
Find my Passion Exercise

1. Look for the happy moments in your life. What feelings were you experiencing during those moments? What made those moments great and special?
2. What kind of hobbies do you have? What do you feel when you indulge in them? How important are they for you? What values do they bring to you?
3. What do you usually think about the most?
4. What do you watch on TV the most? Or what do you search the internet for most of the time? What kind of books and magazines interest you?
5. What inspires you the most and never fails?
6. What topic can you talk about for hours that gets you all excited and animated while talking?
7. What kind of advice do your friends seek from you?
8. What do you talk to yourself about?
9. If you were financially solid and all your financial obligations were met, what would you spend the extra money on? Why?
10. What topics do you care about to the extent of knowing the minutest details?
11. What talents do you have?
12. What are you passionate about?
13. What is easy for you that seems difficult for others to do?
14. What brings a smile to your face?
15. What activities make you lose track of time?

16. What did you enjoy doing when you were a child?
17. What were some of your best skills when you were a child?
18. What could you do for a few years without getting paid?
19. On what subjects do your friends come to you for an opinion?
20. If you were to teach someone to do something, what would it be?

These are some of the questions that can help you establish a sense of passion and purpose. There will be some common answers throughout this exercise. Pay attention to those words that are repeated and check if they resonate with you or not. Be curious about yourself. Ask yourself more questions, similar to the ones above. You can also ask your friends and family members for their opinions about you. You will learn more about yourself when you start being curious about yourself.

This exercise might make you realize that you have more than one passion. That's okay; in fact, it's very exciting. For example, throughout my journey, I have made helping people and educating them my purpose. I also have a passion for cooking, flying, and entrepreneurship. That's where prioritizing comes in; it is very important to get a sense of clarity and direction. Flying liberates my soul and it sets me free — no boundaries, no limits. Cooking adds spice to my life. I enjoy feeding people and having guests over. I have a soft spot for education, too, and I constantly educate myself by reading books or signing up for a class. Entrepreneurship is what makes me alive, and living on the edge is what keeps me going. So, which one should I concentrate on and make a living out of? Can I do two or more? Can I combine two or more? Can I start with one now and start a second later? Those are some of the questions I faced after finding my passion and purpose. When you reach this stage, keep exploring and dig deeper into your vision. There is always more to see in it. After you compile your ideas on that piece of paper, keep it handy for future reference.

Now, on to Exercise 2.

Exercise 2
   My Skill Set Exercise

Strong Skills	Mediocre Skills	Weak Skills
1.	1.	1.
2.	2.	2.
3.	3.	3.
4.	4.	4.
5.	5.	5.
6.	6.	6.

The second exercise is to make a list of your skills. In the strong skills section, you can include everything that you know you are good at. This can account for academic studies, experience, social relationships, hobbies ... etc. This skillset is what will help you deliver your business values. In the second column, we are looking for skills and knowledge that can be described as sufficient or mediocre. For example, troubleshooting computers and the internet is a skill that I have, but I'm not really the best guy to ask for help when it comes to resolving major problems. I know what I know and that's it. I don't even have the necessary knowledge to teach it. Write down all the mediocre skills that you have, and don't think too much about their importance right now. In the last column, we will write down the skills that really need attention and development. This can be a good area to empower your intellectual domain — by educating yourself more about these weak skills. For this exercise, we want to have as many as possible, so the best way to do this is to just let it flow. Don't stop the thinking process by analyzing right now. We will get to that later. Again, keep that answer sheet handy for future reference.

Now that we have gone through the two exercises and have a better idea about our passion, our purpose, and the sets of skills that can help us throughout the journey, we will go on another journey to meet your inner leader. First, I want you to listen to yourself and pay attention to the leader that lives inside of you. We are trying to wake them up and summon them to help you become the future you. Try to visualize the leader and be very clear about every single detail in that image. You have to be connected to their feelings, their vision, their energy level, and their entire being. The inner leader is the best version of you in the future. Try to allow the leader inside to give you a taste of how you would look in the future if you were to live your life as a leader today.

Let's try the following exercise so we can meet the inner leader inside you. First, read the questions. Then close your eyes and connect with that leader to get the answers to this visual exercise.

I want to take you to the future where you are ALREADY accomplished, have achieved your goals, and already have it all. The visualization starts with you being in that state of mind. It has nothing to do with the journey and how you got there. What is important is to imagine that you are there ALREADY! Pay attention to your thoughts and feelings while you are in that stage.

Now, close your eyes and try to answer the following questions:

Hint: If you can record the questions so you can play them back while doing the exercise, it will be a lot better. Leave enough space between the questions to allow you time to think.

Exercise 3
Meet my Inner Leader Exercise

1. Who are you at that moment (in the future)?
2. Where are you? Describe your environment.
3. What are you doing?
4. What are you saying?
5. How do you speak?
6. Whom are you talking to?
7. What are your habits now?
8. What is your daily life like?
9. What activities consume your life now?
10. How did you get there? What have you done to get there?
11. Who is your audience and how do you reach them?
12. How are you delivering your message to the world now? Through a business? A nonprofit organization? Anything else?
13. What are you contributing to the world now?
14. What are you responsible for?
15. How are you serving your audience?
16. What values are you bringing to the world?
17. What is important for you and what do you stand for?
18. How are those values changing your audience's lives?
19. How are you impacting people now?
20. What have you changed in this world?

It is very important to spend enough time with this exercise to answer all the questions thoroughly. Take as much time as you need. But make sure that your answers are truthful and resonate with you.

Another tool to help you connect further with your inner leader is to educate yourself more about a specific role model in your life; try to find the qualities and values that helped them become who they were meant to be. Humans learn quickly by storytelling. If you read stories about your favorite role models, you will gain different perspectives and learn about the characteristics, qualities, and values they embraced and how they used those values to become future leaders. You'll be making a list of the most important ones.

The second part of this exercise is to envision yourself 10 years from now and think about your future qualities and characteristics. Spend time exploring the values that you will be honoring and write everything down on a separate list.

Now look at both lists and compare them with each other and:

1. See what stands out for you?
2. What can you combine, prioritize or take off the list?
3. Spend some time thinking about those characteristics and values from the perspective of both your

role model and yourself. How did these qualities and values help your role model become successful? And how are those qualities and values going to help deliver your message?

After you do the comparison and finalize your list, you will end up with a list of characteristics that will dictate the future you, along with the new set of values that you will be honoring every day.

Exercise 4
Characteristics and Values Exercise

Use the following table to help you gather the necessary information about the characteristics and values of your inner leader and your role model.

My Inner Leader:	My Role Model:
Characteristics:	Characteristics:
1.	1.
2.	2.
3.	3.
4.	4.
5.	5.
Values:	Values:
1.	1.
2.	2.
3.	3.
4.	4.
5.	5.

After you have noted down all the characteristics and values for both parties, take a look at them and combine them into one list of characteristics and values. You can merge them all or filter through them. It is up to you and how you perceive yourself in the future. Pay extra attention to the values you list. You will take each one of them and reflect on the four powers — faith, heart, health, and mind — in order to see where you stand with them in respect to each of your values. This takes us to the Value Application Status Exercise.

Exercise 5
Value Application Status Check Exercise

Name of the value: _____

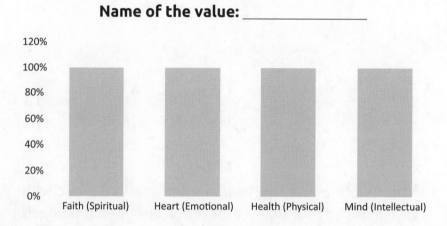

In this exercise, you will take one value at a time and try to put a percentage to its relation to each of the four powers (spiritual, physical, emotional, and intellectual). For example, let's take the value of PROACTIVITY.

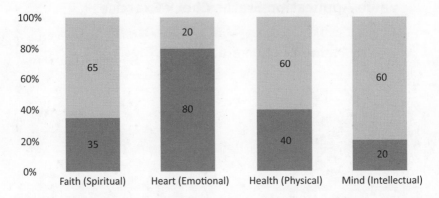

Name of the value: <u>PROACTIVITY</u>

In the figure above, we compare our level of proactivity in each of the four major aspects of our lives. (I plugged in different values randomly to explain the exercise; they don't reflect my reality.) I would like you to take the values that you put on your list and do a chart for every one of them. This will give you an understanding of where you are with each value. Take a deep breath, stand up, shake off all your thoughts and be present when you try to quantify your relationship with all those powers. It is not an exact science, so the percentage is just a rough estimate. Let's do the PROACTIVITY exercise together.

In the first column, the faith department, let's say that you put 35 percent because you don't feel like you are really in touch with your faith that much. So now ask yourself how being at 35 percent is going to help you through the journey. Is 35 percent solid enough to rely on in case I hit rock bottom? How is that 35 percent going to provide support when I need it? What is the impact of having my faith level at 35 percent? How do I feel about that? Where do I want to raise it to? What would it take to make it increase? What is it that I need to do to start moving this 35 percent to 36 percent today?

You should be very curious about your present state and about how you can elevate those feelings and maintain them. To honor the value of proactivity from the faith perspective, you probably need to go to a mosque, church, synagogue, temple or yoga class — or even spend time with nature. Whatever represents spirituality to you, make the extra effort to connect with it again. Consciously work toward reaching 100 percent, even if it might seem like a dream. That's how you apply proactivity as a value to live by.

From an emotional perspective, how can you be proactive? Think about relationships at all levels. Examine your relationships, whether at home with your family members, with your friends, with colleagues at work, professionals in the industry, or people in your neighborhood, your city, the world. What can you do to empower those relationships? Fulfill a promise? Pay more attention when needed? Make someone happy? Try to fix broken relationships? There are many ways to be proactive to make or keep that heart happy. Ask yourself the same questions you did in the faith department.

The third one is very obvious, I believe. Basically, go to the gym, watch what you eat, drink a lot of water, do your medical check-ups, see your dentist, the whole nine yards. I believe we are all familiar with this theme. That's how you reach higher scores in health — by doing the right thing for yourself.

The last one is the intellectual aspect. Let's say that you ranked yourself at 20 percent. That means you need to start getting your mind going because it has been idle for 80 percent of the time. Again, ask yourself the same questions. What needs to be done to get the brain to go to *its* gym so it can warm up and start growing brain muscles? Well, read, read, read, and read some more. Read a book, join a class, play mind developing games like chess. Chess is a great strategy game, and you can play it any time you want if you've got a computer. Ask yourself, how are you honoring the value of being pro-active in the intellectual department?

Now through this exercise for each of your values. This will help you gain more perspective and understanding of what you need to do in your life to become who you are meant to be. The point here is to show consistency across the four dimensions. Take every value and see how it is being honored in each one. That should give you an idea of where you stand with your values and how much you are living by them.

Exercise 6
Life Purpose Statement Exercise

It is now time to start working on your life purpose statement. This is the exercise that my coach, Moustafa Hamwi — the Passionpreneur, used to help me find my purpose. Since he and all our Passionpreneur community believe in paying it forward, I'm sharing an adjusted version of it with you. Hopefully you too will pay it forward so that we can jointly spread more passion and purpose in the world.

I want you to look at the answer sheets that you just came up with and spend some time connecting with your responses. Create that future character now and get clearer about this image. We will use the information from the previous exercises to draft your life purpose statement. You can also call it a personal mission statement or a personal vision statement. What's important is that it captures the essence of who you are and what you will do in this life. This is what your life purpose statement looks like:

My Life Purpose Statement
I, **(your name)**, hereby declare before myself, others, and the universe that my passion and purpose in life is that:

I am the **(The Who)**_____.

I have a life that is full of **(The Life)**_____.

I'm doing this through a _____
(business, for-profit or nonprofit organization, etc.)
that will help **(My Audience)** _____
to **(The How)** _____ so they can
(The Value) _____.

And in the process of all that, I'm **(The Impact)**_____
_____.

I'm enduring pleasure and pain on the journey of making it happen, and I'm loving every single minute of it.

Signed **(Your Signature)** Date **(Future Date)**

Now, before you fill it in, let's discuss the components of the personal life purpose statement and how to use them.

The components

1. **The Who:**
    This is the person you will become.
    Who will you become? Identify that person. Use the answer from question #1 from the MEET THE LEADER exercise.

2. **The Life:**

   What will your life look like? What will it be full of? What will you do to empower the state of your being? What kind of activities will you be doing to keep you focused on your purpose and passion? Use answers 2–10 to give you an idea about how to fill in this section.

3. **The How:**

   Who is your audience? How are you planning to deliver your message? Are you doing it through a business? A non-profit organization? ... etc. Use answers 11–15 to gain insight.

4. **The Values:**

   What values are you bringing to your audience? Use answers 16 and 17 for this part. In addition, use the answers from Exercise 4 (CHARACTERISTICS AND VALUES EXERCISE).

5. **The Benefits of Values:**

   What are the consequences to your audience of embracing the values that you are bringing to the world? Use answer 18 to explain this.

6. **The Impact:**

   What impact are you causing in this world? Use answers 19–20 for this.

Now that we have all the components ready, let's plug them into the personal life statement formula to see how it resonates with you. The life purpose statement will constantly change as you grow. The more you learn, the more opportunities you will discover. So remember to update your personal life statement once in a while to ensure that you are aligned with your progressive thoughts at all times.

Here is how my life purpose statement looked in its initial stages. You can use it as an example to help you come up with your own:

I, _Abbood Tamimi_, hereby declare before myself, others, and the universe that my passion and purpose in life is that:

I am _"The soulpreneur who empowers abused entrepreneurs to become future leaders._ I have a life that is _geared toward advancing human life. I will do that through coaching, mentorship, authoring books, online classes, leading workshops, and public speaking. I will capitalize on my social relationships and will exercise daily to be fit for that life._ I'm doing this through _an organization that will help and invest in aspiring entrepreneurs._ They will become _successful entrepreneurs_, so they can _live a life of their choice and become who they want to be._ And in the process of all of that I'm _creating a generation of free and creative souls who can dictate their destinies and lead the world._

I am enduring pleasure and pain on the journey of making it happen, and I'm loving every minute of it!

Signed: _Abbood Tamimi_ Date: _05/21/2025_

Now that you have your personal life purpose statement drafted, look at it and make it the compass that will dictate your behavior and your direction. You now know what the results look like and what kind of person you need to be to reach the outcome you desire. Let it sink in completely. We will walk the path of becoming a _Soulpreneur_ in my next book. In it you will learn and understand the importance of aligning the purpose of your soul with the purpose of your business.

Conclusion

The mark of true wealth is determined by how much one can give away.

— T. Harv Eker

Congratulations! You have made it to the end.

The journey toward a fulfilling and meaningful life through entrepreneurship is one worth discovering. This book will help you observe your behavior, reflect on your understanding of the world around you, and push you toward finding your purpose and passion.

This book has addressed personal development because entrepreneurship starts with you, not the product or the service you will be offering. To become an entrepreneur, you need to work on yourself first. You need to have clarity about your mission, your purpose, and the message you want to deliver and share with this world. Having clarity is the compass to establish your direction. Similarly, once you get clear about your destination, you will be able to start a business that will complement your mission. This book has shown you how to create your personal life purpose statement; it has also shown you how this statement can be converted to your business' mission and vision statements. That's when you start enjoying the power of aligning your personal values and purpose with your business' values and mission. This is the biggest reason why you need to work on yourself first — because it is you who will deliver the message through your business. If you are not clear about that, the business won't have a clear mission either.

Part of gaining clarity about yourself and your purpose is understanding all the four dimensions that make you a human being and the powers associated with developing them. In this book, we looked at the four main powers that will assist you during your transformational journey.

The power of faith:
We use the power of faith to define your value system and the personal beliefs from which you derive your principles. Your faith is your comfort zone. It's a place that you go to when life shuts its doors in your face. It is also a place where you find your purpose and renew your vows and commitments.

The power of the heart:
The power of the heart will help regulate the way you love yourself, your family, your partner, your friends,

your colleagues, your coworkers, your future clients, your neighbors, your society, and eventually your whole world. Your heart is the lens through which you see and understand people better. It is also the tool that can help filter your emotions to maintain your sanity.

The power of health:
Health power through physical fitness is vital to living longer so you can enjoy a fulfilling life. Exercising is not going to make you successful; it's the consequences of exercise that will help you reach success. It is the habits that you will develop through exercising — such as commitment and organization — that will help you through the rocky road of entrepreneurship.

The power of mind:
The brain is the center of intelligence, through which one can understand the world and how it works. The mind can help manifest your ideas and make them come alive. It is important to understand that this power can enrich your ideas and vision; this will take your intellectual domain to another level.

Change doesn't come easily; it requires a lot of determination and commitment. It is natural to experience resistance at the beginning and sometimes throughout a transformational journey. We all create self-limiting beliefs and other reasons to stay in our comfort zone. But growth doesn't happen when we stay "comfortable." We grow to meet the challenges ahead of us. The more we are challenged, the more we grow. In this book, I have shared the limiting beliefs that made me resistant to change. My personal growth began when I started to step outside my comfort zone.

The Soul Warrior is my mission to help liberate as many trapped souls as I can. I want to help create a generation of free souls who have the vision and the will to become who they choose to be by living a purposeful and fulfilling life. It's the first step you need to take — finding your life's purpose. Then you can align it with your business' purpose to become a successful *Soulpreneur*, which we will discuss in my next book.

It will mean the world to me to hear your stories. I would like to learn about the positive impacts that you choose to make in your life as a result of allowing your soul to lead. Please don't hesitate to reach out and share your stories. You will find my contact information in the "Author Biography" section.

I'm truly humbled that you chose to learn from my story, and I feel blessed that I'm sharing my knowledge to be of service to others.

Now that you have a clear understanding about the big picture, I want you to start implementing your new strategies as soon as possible. Every second that passes won't come back.

I would like you to gain the courage and the will to turn your life into a gift that will be a beacon of light to guide others to create their own legends. Start with small steps. Start with what you have. Start with exercising. Whatever it is, NEVER STAY IDLE.

References

Baumeister, Roy F., Kathleen D. Vohs, Jennifer L. Aaker, and Emily N. Garbinsky. "Some Key Differences between a Happy Life and a Meaningful Life." Taylor & Francis, August 20, 2013. https://www.tandfonline.com/doi/full/10.1080/17439760.2013.830764#preview.

Charles, Shawna. "The 5 Mental Benefits of Exercise." 5 Mental Benefits of Exercise | Walden University.

Collins, James C. 2001. *Good to Great: Why Some Companies Make the Leap ... and Others Don't.* New York: HarperBusiness.

Covey, S. R. 2004. *The 7 Habits of Highly Effective People: Restoring the Character Ethic.* New York: Free Press.

"Did All Prophets Work As Shepherds?" Questions On Islam, https://questionsonislam.com/question/did-all-prophets-work-shepherds

Frankl, Viktor. 2000. *Man's Search for Meaning*. New York: Houghton, Mifflin.

Gordon, S. "Why Does Obesity Cause Diabetes?" MedicineNet. https://www.medicinenet.com/script/main /art.asp?articlekey=39840

Lucchetti, Giancarlo, Alessandra L.G. Lucchetti, Harold G. Koenig. "Impact of Spirituality/Religiosity on Mortality: Comparison With Other Health Interventions," *EXPLORE*, Vol. 7, Iss. 4, (2011), Pages 234–238, http://www.sciencedirect.com/science/article/pii/ S1550830711001029

Mackey, Sean. "Viewing Pictures of a Romantic Partner Reduces Experimental Pain: Involvement of Neural Reward Systems," *PLoS ONE*, Vol. 5 (October 10), https://www.researchgate.net/publication/47520879_ Viewing_Pictures_of_a_Romantic_Partner_Reduces_ Experimental_Pain_Involvement_of_Neural_Reward_ Systems

Montessori, M. 1986. *The Discovery of the Child* (Later Printing ed.). Ballantine Books.

Rinpoche, Sogyal. 2009. *The Tibetan Book of Living and Dying: The Spiritual Classic & International Bestseller: Revised and Updated Edition*. Harper Collins.

Websites:
https://www.rd.com/culture/benefits-of-reading/

https://www.realsimple.com/health/preventative-health/
benefits-of-reading-real-books

https://technologyadvice.com/blog/marketing/1990s-vs-
2017-marketing-then-and-now-infographic/

https://www.slideshare.net/briansolis/official-slideshare-
for-whats-the-future-of-business/2-INFLUENCE
COMES_FROMTHOSE_WEKNOW

https://www.thedailypositive.com/12-reasons-why-you-
should-seek-embrace-change/

Acknowledgments

It took me about two years to write this book. It was an exciting journey on its own. It also took many cups of tea, lots of blank papers, a few pens, pencils, a laptop, a PC, various iWhatever voice recording applications, and many hours in airplanes to bring this book into existence. Moreover, many people have played multiple roles in my life to shape the stories within the stories you will read in this book. Without them, *The Soul Warrior* would not exist.

I want to thank:

- My sister, Rehab. You are my real source of inspiration, determination, and strength. Thank you for being my protector when I was a little kid. You were always by my side when I needed it. You are my guardian angel. Love you!!

- My brother Ahmad. You are downright crazy, and that's what I love about you. You are the kind of guy that would do whatever it takes to get what you want. Keep that up. Your craziness is part of your success.

— The youngest, Moataz. The little one. You have a way of controlling your emotions, and I have learned that from you. And by the way, I feel like I'm talking to Dad when I talk with you sometimes.

— My little niece, Jana. You are my life. Ever since you were born, you have made life feel like a bowl of cherries. Your compassionate heart makes you adorable. Thank you for being so inspirational at a very young age.

I also want to thank:

— My business partner and my "partner in crime," Themis Violaris. Thank you for your trust and faith in me as your business partner. Thank you for supporting the journey and always pushing forward. We have accomplished a lot together, and I have learned a lot from our journey together. THANK YOU.

— My other business partners, Baret Kouyoumdjian and Stavros Synapalos. None of the company's success could be possible without you guys. Thank you for always creating win-win scenarios for everyone.

- My Mentor – Moustafa Hamwi, the Passionpreneur, and rightly so. Thank you for your guidance and your continuous support. Magic happens when we connect to our passion. We are just starting.

- My coach, Bassem Terkawi. It all started from that conversation at CTI Dubai. I heard what I truly needed to hear to become who I am today. You gave me clarity and boosted my confidence to allow my soul to step forward and take the lead.

- My team. Thanks to every team member who joined me on this journey. Every single one of you has enriched my experience and taught me something new about life and perspectives. Thank you for being outstanding players. We wouldn't be where we are today without your dedication and creativity. Thank you, and I will always be by your side when you need me. That's my promise to you.

- My professional coaching community. It is a great honor to be part of this fantastic community dedicated to propelling human life and making it better. Thank you for all your help and advice. Thank you for being authentic and genuine. Thank you for your noble cause and being real angels on Earth. I couldn't have done it without you all.

— All my relatives, friends, and colleagues. Every one of you has a gift that has helped shape who I am today. Thank you for your love and support.

Last but not least:

I want to thank those who hurt me. Thank you for making me strong. Thank you for giving me a purpose to live for. Without your cruelty, I wouldn't be the strong man that I am today. Without your torture, I wouldn't be so determined to help those who have tasted from the same cup. What you have done in the past clearly explains, today, why I was born and the kind of "training" I needed to go through to be able to be of service to others. And because of that, I forgive you.

I pray that one day you will wake up and realize that you are following the wrong path. I hope you realize that you, too, are a victim of your self-made, hostile beliefs charged by negative emotions. I know deep inside of you there are good men kept hostage.

I also hope you give your soul the chance to help you overcome yourself so you don't continue hurting other people. And if you need help, reach out to me. I will help you.

Testimonials

"Abbood helps you free your soul from past trauma holding you back, so you can find your drive to move forward."

Moustafa Hamwi
The Passionpreneur

"What's very special about Abbood is his ability to connect with people at a very deep level. He is also able to look at the past experience, what people have been through and how all that can be incorporated in the future story they want to write for themselves."

Bassem Terkawi
Executive Leadership Coach

"Abbood has the ability and aptitude to meet his clients' needs and requirements. He recognizes the challenges they need and acts quickly and efficiently to offer the best service and support in all aspects of his business. His enthusiasm and

*charisma are also extremely pleasant, which also defines
him as a great partner and friend."*

Matthew Humphreys
Director of Sales and Business Development
(Europe) at Intellian Technologies

*"It is always a pleasure to spend time with Abbood. A totally
courteous, polite and honorable gentleman, who thoroughly
enjoys his life, in work and leisure. I can only recommend him,
both as a businessman and as a person, and count myself
fortunate in his company."*

Kalliope Economou
Sales Manager at Dualog

*"Abbood has definitely set the difference from day one. His
ability to understand our needs and become a true partner
in success was unmatched. I have no doubt that he can
take your business to the next level. Thank you for your
total support and help. You seriously made a great impact
on our progress."*

Wail Dino
General Manager Operations at
ASSA ABLOY Entrance Systems Saudi

"Ridiculously efficient" *is the phrase that comes to mind
when I think about Abbood. I've had the pleasure of working
with Abbood for several years, collaborating on many
projects together, as One Team. Abbood's ability to juggle*

multiple projects was unlike any I've seen before and made a dramatic difference in the productivity level of our sales. He is not only a perfect coach, but also a Mentor for me."

Eleftheria Papadopoulou
Sales Account Manager in the
Maritime/Shipping sector

Call To Action

First of all, I want to acknowledge your determination in finishing this book. I also hope that you are inspired enough to start writing your own future, today. There is nothing impossible once you put your mind to it.

The next step for you is to take action. Nothing will change unless you initiate the change. You can start applying what you have learned from this book on your own or you can reach out for guidance and mentorship and reduce the learning time. Either way, you need to take the first step.

If you are looking for further coaching and mentorship, you can go to www.abboodtamimi.com where you can find two programs that can further enhance your learning:

1. **The Soul Fitness program:**
   Group coaching
   Before you fly, you must learn to walk! Every day brings with it a new set of challenges. You may become

overwhelmed by them and feel like you're unable to make a difference to your life no matter how hard you try. You might just need to get some perspective on what your mental blocks are and prime your soul to receive the success you ask for. No matter who you are or what your background is, it's possible to break through barriers and achieve what you think is impossible. You only need to know how to prepare the right way. Soul Fitness will introduce you to others on the same journey as you and show you how.

What you will get:

1. Discover the saboteurs that sabotage your thoughts and h old you back.	4. Measure your mental fitness progress with a mobile application.
2. Be introduced to your Sage powers.	5. Learn from your group members' personal experiences.
3. Learn how to intercept your saboteurs, evoke the Sage and create positive reactions.	6. Enjoy 8 group coaching sessions to facilitate learning.

2. **The Soul Warrior program:**
   One-on-one coaching for aspiring entrepreneurs
   The mindset of a Soul Warrior is all about turning the difficulties of your past into the opportunities of

your future. No matter your past, if you're an aspiring entrepreneur, the Soul Warrior will teach you how to look at your setbacks and turn them into skills to use every day.

Soul Warriors are willing to jump in and put all their effort behind their business without fear of criticism or failure.

This program will show you how to begin your journey of self-discovery, meet the best version of yourself, and get acquainted with your inner leader. Push yourself outside your comfort zone and up your game so you can play in the big leagues!

What you will get:

1. Discover your true potential	4. Challenge yourself and set the bar high
2. Define your value system	5. Co-create a strategy and an action plan
3. Gain clarity about your purpose and vision	6. Be held accountable for your own success

Go to www.abboodtamimi.com and start your journey.

About The Author

Abbood is a third-generation entrepreneur. Like many entrepreneurs, Abbood has had setbacks that kept his soul hostage for many years. Encountering abuse as a child, Abbood had no choice but to become a grown-up at the age of eleven. He had to battle self-made and limiting beliefs until he finally found a way to connect to his soul and honor its call — and become the CEO that he is today.

Abbood had his first business (a toyshop) at the age of seventeen, right before starting college in Cairo, Egypt. Three years after that, he moved to the US to finish his bachelor's degree in International Business at Johnson & Wales University. There, he started the Investment Club and was an active member of the American Marketing Association and the Society of Advanced Management. Abbood graduated Summa Cum Laude and was a member of the National Honor Society (Alpha Beta Kappa) and the Silver Key Society. His academic life achievements led to recognition in Who's Who Among American Colleges and Universities in 1998-1999.

After graduation, Abbood spent seven years in the banking industry, where he developed his financial skills and gained experience in banking operations, personal/commercial loans, and corporate banking. He was nominated as a "Top Banker" by Citizens Bank and received the "Excellence Award" from Bank of America.

Having spent time gaining experience in corporate America, Abbood decided to honor the entrepreneur inside him. He started a short-lived software development company with his brother before moving to Qatar to help his late father run the family business, which was eventually liquidated with the family's move to Canada.

Despite these challenging experiences, Abbood rejected the idea of returning to work as an employee. Determined to start another business, he co-founded 3mushrooms Telecom in 2012. In 2019 he received two International Business Excellence Awards in Dubai (SME and MARITIME SHIPPING AND LOGISTICS) for his work with 3mushrooms, where he is currently CEO.

With this success, Abbood has decided to share his knowledge and help other entrepreneurs struggling with their own setbacks to gain control over their lives. Whether the setback is a form of abuse or self-limiting beliefs, Abbood solves the problem by reconnecting entrepreneurs to their soul, so they can lead the life they desire. His drive to be of service to others and to educate like-minded people has led him to become a certified Executive Leadership Coach and a Life Coach.

Abbood is determined to create a generation of free souls able to lead this world by creating businesses that are truly an extension of themselves and their life purpose. This generation will help propel humanity by making decisions based on values rather than financial gain. This is what the world needs today.

To learn more about Abbood and how you can work together, please go to www.abboodtamimi.com.